ALBERT CAMUS

LITERATURE AND LIFE: WORLD WRITERS

Selected list of titles in this series:

Complete list of titles in the series available from the publisher on request

ALBERT CAMUS

Alba Amoia

A Frederick Ungar Book
CONTINUUM · NEW YORK

1989

The Continuum Publishing Company
370 Lexington Avenue
New York, NY 10017

Printed in the United States of America

Library of Congress Cataloging-in-Publication Data

Amoia, Alba della Fazia.
    Albert Camus / Alba Amoia.
        p.   cm. — (Literature and life series)
    "A Frederick Ungar book."
    Bibliography: p.
    Includes index.
    ISBN 0-8264-0442-1
    1. Camus, Albert, 1913–1960—Criticism and interpretation.
    I. Title.   II. Series.
PQ2605.A3734Z54645   1989
848′.91409—dc19   89-512
                                                            CIP

To those who hope

Contents

Introduction

Albert Camus is one of those authors who fascinate us by their lives no less than by their writings. A poor boy from the working-class quarter of Algiers, he became a successful novelist, a literary lion, and Nobel Prize winner, yet scorned the intrigues and pretensions of the Paris literary scene and remained emotionally rooted in the North African soil of his boyhood. Often acclaimed as the moral conscience of his generation, he was an unwavering if sometimes incoherent enemy of tyranny and violence, and a persistent champion of the downtrodden and oppressed. As a journalist, he played a part in the World War II resistance to Nazi occupation; but the political and emotional complexities of the subsequent Algerian independence struggle found him inwardly torn, appalled by the violence and brutality of the conflict, yet incapable of giving a clear lead toward its resolution. His death in a motor car accident in 1960, at the early age of forty-six, left us to wonder what if anything his mature years would have added to the handful of literary and dramatic works on which his posthumous reputation is based.

Camus's chosen place was with those men and women who, by virtue of an iron inner discipline and formidable will to live, succeed in maintaining the light of intelligence and equity even in the worst darkness of war, occupation, clandestine struggle, concentration camps, plague, or forced psychiatric treatment. Standing firm against exploitation, conformism, violence, death, or terrorism, such men offer a living refutation of the "reason of State" that seeks to justify hunger, hypocrisy, trials, and inquisitions as "necessary" and "inevitable." In their struggle for an ideal, they are willing even to sacrifice individual freedom; and they are the only ones, Camus maintains, who will reach their goal, albeit at the cost of finding themselves "strangers" in their own societies. How many people today have the sensation of not belonging to a world that bombards them with such a bewildering assortment of limiting philosophies, theories, and strategies—a world that each day resembles more closely a huge Sisyphean mass tumbling down a slippery slope from the hilltop of their ideals?

Albert Camus is a man who held his head high in the face of desperate human conditions, refusing to genuflect in acceptance of the privations, offenses, and persecutions suffered by men in his time. From childhood, he himself had known what it was to be trapped in hunger and illness; and as an adult, he saw men, women, and children condemned to imprisonment, torment, and death by the forces of Fascism, Nazism, and Stalinism. Rather than seek refuge in the supernatural, however, he chose to look on these horrors as on a *darkness* that would be succeeded by *light*—an alternation that helps a prisoner retain a notion of time and balance and offers a reassuring sense that, though the night is long, there is a tomorrow. Light, for Camus, is a source of strength and a symbol of truth. He bathes his almost mystical obsession with life in *"lumière"*—a word that appears innumerable times throughout his works. Algeria's refulgent sunshine, light so bright that it becomes black and white, the Mediterranean's greenish light, light in the olive trees in Italy, and Florence's gentle, fine light—all bear witness to truth for the man whose only God was in the beauty of nature.

So much has been written and, after almost three decades, continues to be written about the man who was born into an illiterate family and became one of France's greatest literary figures, that one must pause to ask exactly why his work exerts so durable an impact. A judicious evaluation of his novels undeniably suggests that some of the characters are mere "sandwich men" parading ideas, rather than flesh-and-blood human beings. If his theatrical production is considered, nothing extraordinary emerges with the possible exception of *Caligula;* nor are his essays comparable to Jean-Paul Sartre's in style and scope. Yet Camus's fame continues to grow, and an ever increasing number of interested young readers is turning to his works, attracted perhaps by their nihilistic component but also, one hopes, by the power of their moral message.

The greatness of Camus, and the consensus that continues to grow around him, seems to be rooted less in his literary oeuvre as such than in the human being that he was: always his true self and true to himself, regardless of the situation; always correct, honest, and stubborn in his respect for the individual. His personality was simple, straightforward, direct and sure, and the interest he showed in things human was always deep and true.

From reading the numerous critical works about Camus, one gains the impression that he has come to be imprisoned in too many partial, limited affirmations about the man and his work. In labeling him a "moralist," an "existentialist," a "dilettante philosopher," or a "political polemicist," his critics tend to restrict and box in what is actually the lesser part of Camus, the part that sometimes disappoints. Beyond his intellectual conceptions, his political, historical and ideological motivations, there is a greater overall view to be taken of his voluminous literary output—which also encompasses Camus the aesthete, the man who can savor and offer such sensations as only a great artist can provide. He is a painter in words, a creator of ideas, situations, poetic incidents, one whose novels can be read at a sitting and leave the reader with the most vivid of color and sense impressions.

Camus, indeed, is much less of an abstract writer than some of his tortuously reasoning critics would make him out to be. He strove for clarity both in his life and in his writings, asserting that "all our troubles spring from our failure to use plain, clear-cut language." His novels, plays, and essays are full of "his" Algeria, "his" mother, "his" tuberculosis, and the political and social situations he personally lived through. The works themselves, moreover, are closely linked by their recurrent themes and reappearing characters. Thus Camus's thought and style not only have intrinsic form, but they weave a living, personalized, ever moving tapestry that sweeps the reader along by its vigor, richness, and sensibility.

Camus was at his best, perhaps, in those of his writings that most directly echo the passion and intensity of his intrinsically "Mediterranean" temperament and consciousness, traits that accompanied him throughout his life and travels. Algeria, Italy, Spain, France, Greece, and other Mediterranean lands shared a natural and human endowment that qualified them, in Camus's eyes, as parts of a single country of which he felt himself to be preeminently a citizen. Early in his life, he had expressed the hope that the "foolish" boundaries between Italy and France—which, together with Spain, formed "the same nation"—would collapse and disappear. After World War II, he envisaged a "Mediterranean man" who would hold a middle, balancing position between the "Russian man" and the "Atlantic man" and who would refuse alliance with either camp. He also conceived, at a later date, of a federation between France and her overseas territories, with his native Algiers as its capital. Speaking of France's "Arab vocation" and Algeria's "European vocation," he stressed the need for a grafting of the two cultures. Although the concept of a French-Algerian association has since faded, such documents as the "Aspen Manifesto" of 1987, which calls for international cooperation among the countries of the Mediterranean basin, continue to emphasize the affinities of interest, culture, landscapes, and style to which Camus bore vigorous witness.

France has claimed Albert Camus as a member of its literary pantheon, and he was indeed faithful to the genius of France in his rationality, humanism, tenacious individualism, his clear, sober, and classical style, and even his inclination toward a certain dilettantism. An American critic, discovering in Camus's thought an ethical affinity with the Anglo-Saxon mind, maintained that his sense of the tragic went to the heart of the American situation and called him the "great writer American literature has waited for and who never came."[1] To this writer, Camus defies all such attempts at national classification. As the exotic hedonist in search of an ideal sunny commonwealth, a lost motherland lying somewhere in the vicinity of submerged Atlantis, perhaps he may here be proposed as the first distinguished "Mediterranean writer" in world literature.

Chronology

1913   Albert Camus is born November 7 near Mondovi, Algeria, in the French overseas *département* of Constantine, to Lucien Camus, a farm laborer whose ancestors had gone to Algeria from Bordeaux, France, and Catherine Sintès, second of nine children in a poor family from Minorca, Spain.

1914   Lucien Camus is seriously wounded in the World War I Battle of the Marne and dies October 11. Albert and his taciturn mother move to the home of his harsh, imperious maternal grandmother in Belcourt, the poor section of Algiers, where he is brought up in extreme hardship but finds pleasure in swimming, playing soccer, and dancing.

1918   Enters the local boys' school in Belcourt, finishing five years later.

1923   Enters secondary school as a scholarship student.

1930   Camus contracts tuberculosis of the right lung, almost resulting in his death; he nevertheless completes his secondary studies *(Lettres Supérieures)* and goes on to his higher education.

1932   Continues his university studies and publishes four articles in the magazine, *Sud*.

1934   Marries Simone Hié on June 16; the marriage ends in divorce less than two years later. Joins the Communist Party.

1935   Travels to the Balearic Islands of Spain.

1936   Having sustained his thesis on "Christian Metaphysics and Neoplatonism," he receives the *diplôme d'études supérieures* from the University of Algiers, but illness prevents him from continuing with postgraduate studies *(agrégation)* and a university career. Takes his second trip outside of North Africa, traveling to Paris, Czechoslovakia, Germany, Austria, and Italy. With a group of amateur actors in Algiers, he founds the Communist-sponsored Théâtre du Travail. His adaptation of André Malraux's novel, *Le temps du mépris (Days of Wrath),* is the first production, followed by *Révolte*

dans les Asturies (Revolt in Asturias), written by the group.
Begins writing notes for his first novel, *La Mort heureuse (A Happy Death)*, published posthumously in 1971.

1937   Publishes *L'Envers et l'endroit (The Wrong Side and the Right Side* [UK title, *Betwixt and Between*]), essays written during 1935–36 and containing many autobiographical elements. Breaks his ties with the Communist Party. Visits Paris in August, then Embrun (a village in the French Alps), Genoa, Florence, and Fiesole. Returning to Algiers, he founds the Théâtre de l'Equipe in October after the demise of the Théâtre du Travail. Begins writing for the newspaper *Alger Républicain*, producing mainly articles protesting French mistreatment of Algerians.

1939   Publishes *Noces (Nuptials)*, four essays written during 1936–38 that reveal his intense feelings for North Africa.

1940   Goes to Metropolitan France (Bordeaux, Lyons, and Clermont-Ferrand), remaining throughout the period of French military collapse in World War II. On December 3, marries Francine Faure, a mathematician who has come from Oran, Algeria, to join him in Lyons. Journalistic service for the newspaper *Paris-Soir* is terminated for economic reasons.

1941   Camus and his wife return to Oran to teach.

1942   The couple returns to Metropolitan France and takes up residence in Panelier, in the Haute-Loire *département*. Francine returns to Algeria, but the Allied landing in North Africa prevents Camus from leaving Metropolitan France. Publishes his first novel, *L'Etranger (The Stranger* [UK title, *The Outsider*]).

1943   Camus and his wife move to German-occupied Paris. In addition to journalistic work, he finds employment with the important publishing house of Gallimard, where he remains until 1960 as reader and director of its *"Espoir"* collection. Joins the resistance movement. Publishes *Le Mythe de Sisyphe (The Myth of Sisyphus)*, begun in 1939.

1944   Publishes a final version of the drama *Caligula* (the original version had been written in 1938 for the Théâtre de l'Equipe), and *Le Malentendu (The Misunderstanding* [UK title, *Cross Purpose*]), written in 1942–43.

1945   Following the liberation of Paris in 1944, he revives *Combat*, the former resistance newspaper to which he and Jean-Paul

Sartre had contributed leading articles, remaining as editor until 1947. Publishes *Lettres à un ami allemand (Letters to a German Friend)*, written during 1943–44.

1946 Sets out for New York on March 10 for a two-month travel and lecture tour in the United States and Canada.

1947 Publishes *La Peste (The Plague)*, which receives the French Prix de la Critique.

1948 Travels to Algeria in February. The play about a plague, entitled *L'Etat de siège (State of Siege)*, is produced and published in Paris but meets with a cold reception.

1949 Embarks at Marseilles on June 3 for a lecture tour in South America, which ends on August 31. Still suffering from tuberculosis, he goes to rest at Cabris, near Grasse.

1950 Returns to Paris in March. *Les Justes (The Just Assassins)* written in 1948–49, is published. *Actuelles I: Chroniques, 1944–48*, containing articles from *Combat*, is published by Gallimard. Spends the summer in the Vosges Mountains, returning to Paris in September.

1951 Publishes *L'Homme révolté (The Rebel)*, a discussion of the ideology of revolution, which is severely criticized by Jean-Paul Sartre and other leading figures.

1953 Gallimard publishes *Actuelles II: Chroniques, 1948–53*, containing Camus's most polemical articles. Camus adapts and publishes Calderón de la Barca's tragedy, *Devotion to the Cross*, and Pierre de Larivey's comedy, *The Spirits* (1579).

1954 *L'Eté (Summer)*, a collection of lyrical essays written as early as 1939, is published. Camus travels to Italy. The Algerian war for independence from France breaks out on November 1, but Camus refuses comment on the subject.

1955 Delivers a lecture on "The Future of Tragedy" in Athens in May. Adapts for the French stage Dino Buzzati's *An Interesting Case*.

1956 Publishes *La Chute (The Fall)*, a semiautobiographical monologue in the form of a short novel. Takes a trip to Algiers. Adapts for the French stage and publishes William Faulkner's novel, *Requiem for a Nun*.

1957 A volume of short stories, *L'Exil et le Royaume (Exile and the Kingdom)* appears, as does *Réflexions sur la peine capitale (Reflections on Capital Punishment)*, written jointly with Arthur Koestler. Adapts, produces, and publishes Lope de Vega's *Knight of Olmedo*. Receives the Nobel Prize for Literature on December 10, "for his important literary works which shed light on the problems today facing the human conscience."

1958   Gallimard publishes *Actuelles III: Chronique algérienne, 1939–58,* containing most of Camus's writings on Algeria. He travels to Greece, and, in June, buys a home in Lourmarin (*département* of Vaucluse) in southern France.

1959   Publishes his adaptation of Fyodor Dostoyevski's novel, *The Possessed*.

1960   Returning to Paris from Lourmarin, Camus is involved in an automobile accident at Petit-Villeblevin (*département* of Yonne) and dies on January 4 at the age of forty-six. He is buried at Lourmarin. Work in progress at the time of his death includes a novel, *Le premier homme (The first man),* and a play, *Don Juan.*

1962   Camus's jottings of the years 1935–42 are published by Gallimard in the first volume of *Carnets (Notebooks).*

1964   Jottings of 1942–51 are published in the second volume of *Notebooks.*

1967   Dino De Laurentiis produces a film of *The Stranger,* with Marcello Mastroianni and Anna Karina.

1970   Camus's first wife, Simone Hié, dies.

1971   *A Happy Death,* composed in 1937–38, is published posthumously by Gallimard in the first volume of the *Cahiers Albert Camus,* containing the author's early attempts at fiction.

1973   The second volume of the *Cahiers Albert Camus* contains sundry, tentative pieces dating from the years prior to 1934.

1979   Camus's second wife, Francine Faure, dies on December 24, shortly before she was to attend a conference on her late husband's works in Florida.

1989   Third and last volume of *Notebooks* is published by Gallimard.

Part I

The Life

What makes men good is held by some to be nature, by others habit or training, by others instruction. As for the goodness that comes by nature, this is plainly not within our control, but is bestowed by some divine agency on certain people who truly deserve to be called fortunate.

—Aristotle, *Nicomachean Ethics*

1

The Story of His Life

"Sunlight and shadow," *(Soleil et ombre)* is the fitting subtitle of a recent book[1] on Albert Camus, a man and writer whose portrait, still incomplete, is at the same time luminescent and eclipsed, revered and contested. Camus's life and thought must be painted in a chiaroscuro of drenching light and somber darkness, for what he offers is a constant play of opposites: love for the Mediterranean sun, and aversion for the gloom of northern climes; exaltation of Hellenic culture (his "midday"), and deprecation of Europe's "miserable tragedies" (his "midnight"); glorification of life, and watchful struggle against death; and, most importantly, painstaking search for the right side and the wrong side of the human conscience. Camus's conception of man's spiritual makeup as an interplay of opposing forces is neatly illustrated by a well-known caricature of David Levine in which two full figures of Camus, one winged, the other tailed, angel and beast, are closely locked—is it in dance or in deadly battle?

Camus rejoiced and suffered in the contrast between the richness of Algeria's countryside and the misery of its people. Throughout his life he remained keenly aware of the dichotomy between poverty and wealth. He himself had suffered from the indigence of his family, yet had derived abundant nourishment from the sea and the sun, which, as he wrote, "in Africa . . . are free." Seats in the sun in Spanish bullfight arenas cost less than those in the shade, but for Camus they are the better bargain.

He himself was Spanish on his mother's side. Catherine Sintès, the second of nine children, belonged to a poor family that had come to Algeria from Minorca, one of the Balearic Islands. His father, Lucien Camus, a native Algerian, was employed as a farmhand in the vineyards at Chapeau de Gendarme, near Mondovi, a few kilometers south of Bône in what was then the French overseas *département* of Constantine. It was there that Albert Camus was born on November 7, 1913. His father's ancestors had gone to Algeria from Bordeaux, and were among the first of the French settlers who subsequently became known as *pieds-noirs,* either because of the unfamiliar color of their shoes or because they were agricultural laborers and therefore had muddy feet.

Albert was only a few months old when his father, newly drafted into the Algerian-based French infantry corps known as the "Zouaves," was fatally wounded in the World War I Battle of the Marne and died October 11, 1914. Lucien Camus is buried in Saint-Brieuc, France, on the English Channel; Albert Camus visited his grave for the first time in 1947. Of World War I, the younger Camus was to remember only the "beating of drums"; as an adult, he was to offer the pessimistic observation that, following the war, history had continued to consist of a sequence of murders, violence, and injustices.

Though he knew little about his father, Camus always remembered a simple anedocte about him that he had heard in his childhood. A humble, honest, and simple man, Lucien had decided to witness the public execution of a particularly vicious murderer, who, he was convinced, deserved the death penalty. But the sight of the condemned man panting under the blade of the guillotine so affected Lucien that he fled from the scene. Returning home, he refused to speak, threw himself on his bed, and was seized by a fit of vomiting. Camus alludes to this incident three times in his own writings, in the last chapter of *The Stranger,* in *The Plague,* and in "Reflections on the Guillotine."

Catherine Sintès, Camus's mother, was an illiterate, unsmiling, passive, and seemingly indifferent woman who, as her son was later to observe, often "stared abnormally at the floor." A speech defect had relegated her to an attitude of silence that was reinforced by her work as a cleaning woman. After her husband had been shipped off to France, Catherine, with her two sons, Lucien and little Albert, moved into her mother's three-room apartment in Algiers, which already housed her mother and two brothers, all illiterate. Equipped with neither running water nor electricity, the apartment was located in a slum neighborhood that bore the ironic name of Belcourt.

In this unpromising environment, little Albert grew up in abject poverty, suffering malnourishment, physical punishment from his brutal, authoritarian grandmother, and mental anguish in the presence of a tyrannical, jealous, and deaf uncle who harshly interfered in the personal life of Albert's resigned mother. Catherine Sintès and her son communicated only silently in this oppressive ménage. But young Camus did find welcome relief from the bleakness of the apartment in the bright sun and colorful beaches of Algiers. Sunbathing and swimming never failed to fill him with joy and sensuous delight. The contrast between the poverty in which he lived and the splendor of the Mediterranean at his doorstep was to leave a lasting mark on his work.

Albert attended the local boys' school from 1918 to 1923. The generous encouragement of one of his teachers, Louis Germain, who recognized Albert's exceptional intelligence, helped him to stave off his imperious grandmother's insistence that the young boy renounce education and find a job. Germain was also instrumental in obtaining a scholarship for Albert to enter the secondary school that is known today as the Lycée Abd-el-Kader, and which he attended from 1923 to 1930. Professor Jean Grenier, a teacher in the secondary school and a philosopher of some distinction, also took a strong personal interest in him, notwithstanding his initial impression of a somewhat undisciplined student who needed to be seated under his eye in the first row of desks. Subsequently, a strong bond of friendship and mutual intellectual interests developed between them. Grenier, himself a writer of some note, read and criticized (albeit with extreme severity) many of Camus's writings over the years, and published in 1968 a well-known book containing his personal collections of the celebrated author.

At fourteen, Albert became a soccer enthusiast, playing goalkeeper for the junior team of the "Racing Universitaire d'Alger." But after actively and fervidly pursuing the sport for two years, he was forced to desist by the appearance in 1930 of the first symptoms of the tuberculosis that was to plague him throughout his life. Henceforth denied the possibility of active participation, he kept his interest in soccer as a lifelong spectator who learned to experience vicarious enjoyment from his stadium seat. It was to his soccer experience, he later wrote, that he owed his sure sense of morality and duty.

"Caseous pulmonary tuberculosis of the right lung" was the diagnosis of Albert's illness by the physicians at Mustapha Hospital, "the poor neighborhood hospital" of Camus's posthumously published first novel, *A Happy Death* (1971). The illness was chronic and progressive—four years later, the left lung also became involved—and it affected not only Camus's physical well-being, causing fatigue, malaise, drenching perspiration, hemoptysis (blood spitting) and fever, but his entire attitude and thoughts as well. Out of his experience of illness there grew, on the one hand, a philosophical conviction that human existence is, in the words of the German philosopher Martin Heidegger, "being-towards-death"; and, on the other hand, a deep attachment to life that went hand in hand with his reserved detachment from it. The beauty of the Mediterranean landscape, in Italy and elsewhere, would do much "to help him live as well as to help him die."

Convalescence from the first onset of his illness compelled Camus to repeat a year of classes at the secondary school. Professor Grenier, who had noticed his absence, made inquiry and, on learning of his illness, paid the student a visit at his home. But both were painfully embarrassed by the poverty in which the Camus family lived. Conversation proved impossible, and Professor Grenier left almost immediately. The trauma of this incident left its traces throughout Camus's entire life. Not long afterward, the seventeen-year-old Albert was taken into the home of an uncle by marriage, the butcher Gustave Acault, who could give him better food and lodging than his mother could provide. Unlike some other family members, the exuberant Acault was an avid reader, and he was to serve as the nearest approach to a father figure in the youthful Camus's life.

Albert Camus himself was aware from the age of seventeen onward that he wished to become a writer. His first literary experiences were gained as a member of the "North African Literary Group," which met in the Casbah of Algiers to exchange ideas over cups of tea garnished with floating mint leaves and pine seeds. By 1932, he was composing articles for publication in the local magazine *Sud,* writing prolifically on Stendhal, Aeschylus, André Gide, and other authors. In a long poem titled "Méditerranée" (1933), he found language of extreme richness to express his devotion to the sea that "polishes and humanizes" the world. As art critic, he contributed pieces to the newspaper *Alger-Etudiant* during 1934.

In that year, still a minor and still poor, he married Simon Hié, an attractive and well-to-do but unstable girl with a serious drug addiction problem. His Uncle Gustave vigorously opposed the marriage, being unable to imagine how a poor student and a rich girl could make it succeed. His perplexity was in fact resolved less than two years later when, despite Camus's efforts, the marriage disintegrated.

Albert's 1934 Christmas gift to Simone was a handwritten copybook of fairy tales about the legendary medieval figure of Mélusine. To his wife he also dedicated a collection of his impressions from his childhood in Belcourt, "Les Voix du quartier pauvre" (Poor neighborhood voices), which were to become his first published book, *The Wrong Side and the Right Side* (1937).

Camus had entered the University of Algiers in 1932, took his degree in 1935, and in 1936 was awarded the *diplôme d'études supérieures* after successfully sustaining his thesis *(cum laude)* on "Christian Metaphysics and Neoplatonism." In this work, Camus compared Plotinus, the third-century philosopher of Neoplatonism, and Saint Augustine, the bishop of Hippo in North Africa, who was born, like Camus, near Bône, and whose thought was deeply influenced by Plotinus. Camus tried to show in his thesis to what extent Christianity is original as compared to Hellenism, and to what extent Christian thought drew from Greek models.

Camus's own religious outlook is difficult to define with precision. He has been variously labeled an "atheistic humanist," a pagan, a neopagan, a "Christian pagan," and a secular saint. He himself declared that having been born in a pagan land in a Christian era, he felt closer to the values of the ancient world than to Christian ones, for what he had seen of the Catholic religion in his youth in Belcourt was spiritually poor and linked principally to a fear of death rather than a love of life. While respecting Christian faith, he refused to accept its supernatural elements or the concept of human sin and divine malediction. Yet he felt close in spirit to Saint Francis of Assisi, who had turned Christianity into a hymn to nature. He could easily convert to Franciscanism, he wrote in his *Notebooks,* "were it not already [his] religion." He associated God with the Mediterranean in a unique formula in which sun and light emerge as his personal source of truth. Camus had faith in whatever helped him most freely to live the life of the flesh and of the mind; and the morality he chose was based on respect for human life and for the individual. His was a holiness without God.

Camus's first trip outside his beloved Mediterranean region was a visit to Austria, eastern Germany, and Czechoslovakia in June 1936, which coincided with the breakup of his marriage. Far from enjoying the novelty of travel, he longed desperately for his own city and its gentle Mediterranean nights. All that later remained of his visit to Prague, he confessed, was an odor of cucumbers soaked in vinegar, which filled him with anguish. Traveling home via Italy (Venice and Vicenza), he was delighted to find himself again in regions where light and beauty drenched the landscape.

He spent another few days in Fiesole and Florence in the following year, 1937, before returning to Algiers after a sojourn in Paris and in Embrun, a village in the Hautes-Alpes *département* where he spent a month of convalescence from a tubercular attack. Camus found happiness in Tuscany,[2] whose lushness of nature, perfumed air, and deep blue sky aroused in him the same sensual response he had experienced in Algeria.

After receiving his university diploma, Camus should logically have continued his postgraduate studies (the *agrégation*) and a university career. Instead, he toyed with the idea of leaving Algeria for Indochina. In the end, however, his illness precluded both options, although his economic situation left much to be desired. During these years he was employed in a succession of ill-paid posts as meteorologist, automobile parts salesman, government clerk, and maritime stockbroker's agent. His real interest was directed less toward earning a living than toward the pleasures of daily existence—soccer, girls, swimming, and sunning, and, more important, to his future, literature and the theater. Work as an actor with the Radio-Algiers theatrical group, touring the cities and villages of Algeria, provided an apprenticeship in the rudiments of dramatic art. A lasting passion for the theater would find expression not only in his own acting, in his stage adaptations (André Malraux's *Days of*

Wrath, Calderón de la Barca's *Devotion to the Cross,* Pierre de Larivey's *The Spirits,* Dino Buzzati's *An Interesting Case,*[3] William Faulkner's *Requiem for a Nun,* Lope de Vega's *Knight of Olmeda,* Dostoyevski's *The Possessed*), but in his own plays, *Caligula, The Misunderstanding, State of Siege,* and *The Just Assassins.*

With people of the theater, Camus felt happy and relaxed, whereas in intellectual circles, he often chafed. The theater to him was the highest literary genre, and he deemed himself fortunate to be simultaneously writer, actor, and stage director, a combination that permitted him to give a unity of tone, style, and rhythm to what he called the "total drama." It is reported that at the time of his death in 1960 he is understood to have been negotiating with André Malraux, then Minister of State for Cultural Affairs, to take possession of the Récamier Theater in Paris to direct an acting group of his own.

Camus had been strongly influenced by the writings of Jacques Copeau, a theatrical innovator and the founder of the Vieux-Colombier Theater in Paris. For the theater that Camus himself founded in Algiers in 1937, he used Copeau's repertoire extensively; and in the lecture he was to deliver in Greece in 1955 on the subject of the future of tragedy, he makes deferential reference to Copeau's theatrical concepts.

The theater, for Camus, was not only an art form but also a vehicle for political expression. As a man who had himself emerged from the depths of poverty, Camus would retain throughout his life a feeling of solidarity with the oppressed of this earth and a hatred of those who dominated and exploited them. This attitude was to persist without variation through all the changes of political orientation that mark his progress through the troubled decades of the mid-twentieth century—his initial flirtation with Communism, his steadfast opposition to the fascist totalitarianism of Mussolini and Hitler, and his postwar denunciation of the repression and crimes of Stalinist Russia.

The sense of fraternity with the impoverished people of his world extended not only to the European working class in Algeria, to which he himself belonged, but encompassed also the indigenous Muslim Algerians who generally stood even lower in the economic and social scale. It was primarily in a gesture of solidarity with his Muslim contemporaries that Camus became a member of the Communist Party in 1934, just as his departure from the party a few years later was motivated by a shift in the party line that threatened to sidetrack Muslim aspirations in the interest of the new Popular Front policy initiated in Metropolitan France.

In the meantime, Camus had been named secretary-general of the Algiers "House of Culture" launched by the Parisian directorship of the Communist Party, which in turn was to provide the funds for the founding of the theatrical group known as the "Théâtre du Travail." For the inauguration of the House of Culture, on February 8, 1936—the year that marked both the conquest of Ethiopia by Mussolini's fascist troops and the outbreak of the Spanish Civil War—Camus delivered a speech entitled "The New Mediterranean Culture," in which he called for the rise of a nationalism of the Mediterranean sun as opposed to the gloomy darkness of the European dictatorships. (It must be noted that "Mediterranean" for the young Camus is not associated with Roman and occidental Latinity but rather with Greece and the oriental currents of thought. He had no love for ancient Rome and nothing in common with Mussolini's imperialistic conception of the Mediterranean as *Mare nostrum*, our sea.)

The Théâtre du Travail's first production, under Camus's own direction, was the adaptation of André Malraux's *Days of Wrath*, France's first literary work on the subject of Nazism and its horrors. (Malraux, incidentally, had gone to Algiers in 1935 to speak on the threat of fascism in a Belcourt moviehouse.) The two performances of *Days of Wrath*—for the benefit of the unemployed of Algiers— were enthusiastically received, and it is reported that the spectators sang in chorus the Communist hymn, *L'Internationale,* in support of the resistance hero of the play.

The next production of the Théâtre du Travail was to have been *Revolt in Asturias*, a play written by members of the troupe about the workers' insurrection in Oviedo, Spain, in 1934. Rehearsals were interrupted, however, by order of the mayor of Algiers, who banned performances of the play out of an alleged fear of disturbances during an ongoing electoral campaign. The play was nevertheless published in Algiers, and extracts were presented on stage, under the title *Spain 1934*, from April 1937 on, alternating with performances of Maksim Gorki's *Lower Depths*, Ben Jonson's *The*

Silent Woman, Aeschylus's *Prometheus Bound*, Aleksandr Pushkin's *Don Juan* (in which Camus played the title role), and *Article 330*, a play by the French author, Georges Courteline, known for his bitter satire. The star of *Article 330*, the last scene of which shows the protagonist publicly exposing his derrière (anticipating a well-known scene in *Last Tango in Paris*), was none other than Albert Camus.

Camus had not felt at ease amid the bureaucratic rigidities of the Communist movement. His break with the party, probably in the spring of 1937, coincided with the collapse of the House of Culture and the demise of the Théâtre du Travail. Nothing daunted, Camus founded in October 1937 his own theatrical troupe, the Théâtre de l'Equipe, which provided the opportunity to dedicate himself to Copeau's repertory rather than spending time on politico-revolutionary plays. Feeling freer to follow his own direction and inspiration in his theatrical initiatives, he played in 1938 in Charles Vildrac's *The Good Ship Tenacity* as well as in Jacques Copeau's adaptation of *The Brothers Karamazov*, and, in 1939, in John Synge's *The Playboy of the Western World*, the last play to be presented by the Théâtre de l'Equipe before its closing due to the darkening international situation.

These theatrically active prewar years also saw the publication of the collection of short pieces already referred to, *The Wrong Side and the Right Side* (1937) and the composition (1936–38) of *Nuptials* (published in 1939), a collection of four essays: "Noces à Tipasa" ("Nuptials at Tipasa"); "Vent à Djemila" ("Wind at Djemila"); "Le Désert" ("The Desert"), recording Camus's impressions of Florence and Fiesole; and "L'Eté à Alger" ("Summer in Algiers"). While the tone of *The Wrong Side and the Right Side* is somber and desolating, *Nuptials* is bright, lyrical, and exotic, and conveys a feeling that Camus is now sure of his literary vocation.

Even while writing *Nuptials*, Camus was making notes for his first novel, *A Happy Death*, which, however, was interrupted or rather shunted aside by his work on *The Stranger* and was not published until after the author's death. *The Stranger* (1942) is, however, essentially an outgrowth of *A Happy Death*, and much has been written concerning the relationship between the two novels. *The Stranger* marked Camus's emergence as a full-fledged writer; it was to remain one of his masterpieces and has become a universally known classic.

In the meantime, Camus had begun to earn his living as a journalist on *Alger Républicain*, a new, liberal, antifascist newspaper whose director, a Parisian intellectual by the name of Pascal Pia, was to become Camus's firm friend, although he would detach himself years later because of the divergence of their ideas and temperaments. Camus's contributions consisted mainly of literary criticisms and protests against social injustices, especially the pervasive discrimination against the Muslim Algerians. Of major importance was his meticulously documented eleven-article series on the famine in Kabylia, the high country south of Algiers, which appeared in June 1939 and was republished in *Actuelles II* in 1958. It vividly reflects Camus's personal involvement and his vicarious participation in the inhabitants' misery and hunger, to the point where he was unable to enjoy the beauty of nature surrounding him.

Camus's application to join the army on the outbreak of World War II was rejected for reasons of health, and his employment by *Alger Républicain* was terminated by the closing of that newspaper as a result of official disapproval of its position on North African problems. Returning to Paris, his friend Pia took a position on the newspaper *Paris-Soir* and obtained a post for Camus as well. A grateful Camus arrived in Paris in March 1940; but the city proved to be a place of exile for him, one in which he felt ill at ease and sorely missed his Mediterranean sun. Paris, like all of Europe, seemed to him mechanized and convulsed, lacking in true humanism.

His feelings of sadness and isolation deepened even more when the fall of France and the German occupation of Paris forced *Paris-Soir* to transfer its offices to the unoccupied zone, first to Clermont-Ferrand, then to Lyons—colorless, gray, central, sea-less regions where he was possessed by a kind of claustrophobia. He would later describe these parts of France as resembling hell, with their "endless gray streets and everyone dressed in black."

Despite the uncertainties of the times and the precariousness of his position with *Paris-Soir*, Camus was married for the second time on December 3, 1940, to Francine Faure, a mathematics specialist from Oran, Algeria, who came to join him in Lyons. The civil ceremony was of the simplest: five friends attending, and a bouquet of violets as a wedding gift. Less than a month later, Camus's journalistic service for *Paris-Soir* was terminated for economic reasons. Albert and Francine had no alternative but to return to Oran, where both found teaching positions. The hot Algerian summers, however, proved detrimental to Camus's health; and he found Oran to be a hideous city, one in which he again felt he was living in forced exile. (Oran would be the city Camus chose to describe in *The Plague*.) Eventually the couple was able to obtain safe conduct to return to Metropolitan France in the summer of 1942. They took up residence in Panelier, in the Hautes-Alpes *département*, where Francine's family had often visited and where the cool mountain air was beneficial to Camus's lung condition.

The Stranger, Camus's first novel, had meanwhile appeared in Paris in June 1942, to be followed only four months later by *The Myth of Sisyphus*, the philosophical treatise at which he had been working since 1940. Francine had meanwhile returned to Oran, where Camus had intended to join her in November 1942; but the Allied landings in North Africa and the German invasion of southern France prevented him from leaving, and the couple remained separated until the liberation of France almost two years later.

Camus returned to German-occupied Paris in November 1943 as a reader for the important publishing house of Gallimard. At about the same time, he began contributing various texts and articles to the resistance press, notably the "Letters to a German Friend," written during 1943–44, which were published in book form in 1945. In these four letters to an imaginary correspondent, Camus seeks to establish a system of higher human values worth living, fighting, and dying for, as opposed to the blind Nazi mystique of a strong state. The third letter propounds a notion of Europe vastly different from the Nazi-dominated Europe of Hitlerite propaganda: an agglomeration of "free Europeans" such as was later to crystallize in the concept of the European Communities. By late 1943 or early 1944, his friend Pascal Pia had also involved him in the editing of the clandestine *Combat*, the leading resistance newspaper, to which Jean-Paul Sartre and other prominent intellectuals were contributing.

While still living in Algiers before the outbreak of war, Camus had begun work on a drama, *Caligula,* which was to have been presented at the Théâtre de l'Equipe with himself as the mad Roman emperor. Published in 1944 and first performed at the Théâtre Hébertot in Paris in 1945 with Gérard Philipe in the title role, the play was seen by Camus as completing what he called his "three Absurds": the novel, *The Stranger;* the essay, *The Myth of Sisyphus;* and *Caligula,* an illustration of how supreme political power, or liberty subject to no restrictions, can lead to devastating self-destruction. *Caligula* proved to be Camus's most durable theatrical success.

In the meantime, a second drama, *The Misunderstanding*—Camus's "modern tragedy"—was completed and performed in Paris in June 1944, only days before the withdrawal of the German occupying force. The role of Marthe, the cold-blooded murderess who longs for the warm South, was played by Maria Casarès, a young Spanish actress to whom Camus became deeply attached and with whom he carried on an intermittent love affair for the rest of his life.

The liberation of Paris made it possible for *Combat* to emerge as France's most prestigious "legitimate" newspaper, with Pascal Pia as director and Camus as managing editor and a regular contributor. Despite its self-consciously proclaimed aim of replacing politics by morality and using information as the "key of democracy," the paper was lively and intelligent, with Sartre, Simone de Beauvoir, André Gide and other notable writers among its contributors. Many of Camus's own contributions were later collected in the volume entitled *Actuelles I,* a chronicle of the years 1944–48 that was published in 1950 and permits the reader to observe Camus's search for a tenable ideological position amid the new perplexities of the East–West "Cold War."

Francine, Camus's wife, arrived from Algeria in October 1944, and twins, a boy, Jean, and a girl, Catherine, were born September 5, 1945. Camus's genuine fondness for Francine and for his children did not, however, entirely supplant the Bohemian way of life and multiple love affairs to which he had become accustomed ever since his early years in Algeria.

At the Gallimard publishing house, Camus had by now become director of the *"Espoir"* collection, and his name was beginning to be well-known among French intellectuals. His editorship of *Com-*

bat terminated in June 1947, as a result of general fatigue and growing conflict with Pascal Pia; but the publication of his new novel, *The Plague,* during the same year, brought immediate and immense success, both literary and financial. With the substantial royalties received from his novel, Camus felt impelled to settle an old debt to the University of Algiers. As a poor student, he had obtained loans to continue his studies; he now repaid them, fifteenfold.

Among those most impressed by *The Plague* was Jean-Louis Barrault, the celebrated actor and director, who had been working on a theatrical adaptation of Daniel Defoe's *A Journal of the Plague Year* (1722) and now sought Camus's collaboration for a play on the theme. Working together closely, Barrault and Camus produced in *State of Siege* (1948) a so-called total drama that uses a completely different setting and stresses the political dimensions of revolt and denunciation of totalitarian systems. But despite Camus and Barrault, a brilliant cast, and the incidental music of Arthur Honegger and miming of Marcel Marceau, the play proved to be as resounding a failure as *The Plague* had been a success.

Nor did anything come of Camus's later idea of modifying *State of Siege* and staging it outdoors in Greece—the cradle of philosophy, his ideal land, the country that symbolized for him nature, beauty, culture, and civilization. Years earlier, he had drafted a series of notes on ancient Greece in preparation for a trip he had planned with Francine Faure in August 1939, but which had been canceled because of the war. The twenty-day trip that eventually materialized in 1955—to Athens, Epidaurus, Nauplia, Mycenae, Delphi, Mykonos, Delos, Olympia, and Aegina—filled Camus's "Greek heart" with "sacred inebriation."

Two much less intoxicating voyages preceded the Greek trip. The first, in 1946, was to North America, where Camus, despite his status as a government-sponsored lecturer, was briefly refused entry at Ellis Island as a somewhat suspect leftist journalist. Elsewhere in the United States he was known mainly as a resistance writer and for his resemblance, in his rumpled beige raincoat with cigarette dangling from his lips, to Humphrey Bogart. The second trip, this time to South America in 1949, was a lonely, depressing, and disappointing adventure that weakened him physically and mentally, causing him briefly but seriously to contemplate suicide. The stories of these two trips, recorded impressionistically in Camus's *Notebooks,* were subsequently extracted and published separately in 1978 as *Journaux de voyage* (first English translation, *American Journals,* 1987).

At the end of 1949 came the premiere of Camus's fourth play, *The Just Assassins,* a study of the Russian revolutionaries of 1905, which opened at the Théâtre Hébertot on December 15 with Maria Casarès in the role of the idealistic female terrorist.

This drama was an outgrowth of Camus's work on his lengthy essay, *The Rebel* (1951), in which he tries to evoke a political philosophy consistent with his generous social impulses, his concern for justice and freedom, his hatred of violence, and his revulsion against the cynical opportunism of many organized political movements—particularly those of a totalitarian character. But when his analysis was finally published, it came under attack from all sides. While André Breton and the surrealists took issue with Camus's "conformism" and his doctrine of "revolt with moderation," his erstwhile friend Sartre, at that time a defender of Soviet Communism, denounced "Camus the bourgeois" in his well-known magazine, *Les Temps modernes,* in terms that provoked a serious politico-philosophical dispute and ultimately led to a complete break between the two men.

This quarrel between two of France's leading men of letters reflected a basic disagreement with regard to Marxism and Soviet Communism. As an apologist for the Stalin regime, Sartre argued that injustices were sometimes unavoidable and must be tolerated, whereas Camus, as champion of individual freedom, refused to condone Stalinist terrorism. Some recent critics have seen in the latent antagonism between the two men a sociological element arising from their differing social origins, Sartre the bourgeois and Camus the man of the working class. It has even been suggested that Camus's physical attractiveness and the fascination he possessed for women stirred the antipathy of the ugly and almost deformed Sartre.[4] The two distinguished writers were never to see each other after the break between them, although Sartre paid homage to Camus when he learned of his death, and he himself rejected further collaboration with the Communists in 1970.

Another book of essays—this one lyrical and Mediterranean in character like *Nuptials*—was published in 1954 under the title

Summer. Written over a prolonged period extending from 1939 to 1953, *Summer* consists of eight essays, all inspired by the Mediterranean sun. Most celebrated are "Le Minotaure ou la halte d'Oran" ("The Minotaur or A Stop at Oran"); "Retour à Tipasa" ("Return to Tipasa"); and "La Mer au plus près" ("The Sea Up Close"), a highly poetic and imaginative declaration of love to the sea, inspired in part by his transatlantic trips.

Camus's last novel, *The Fall* (1956) is a complex, ironical, and semiautobiographical monologue which some critics consider his best work. Originally intended as one of the short stories in the collection entitled *Exile and the Kingdom* (1957), it became instead an independent book whose narrator denounced himself with acuity and ferocity. In *Exile and the Kingdom*, a work that had been gestating since 1952, the theme of exile is treated in a variety of ways depending on whether the exile is geographical or moral in character.

Also in 1957, Camus and Arthur Koestler published their dual volume, *Reflections on Capital Punishment*. The two authors had met in 1944 at the Saint-Germain-des-Prés debates of Sartre, Simone de Beauvoir, and their group. Koestler's "Reflections on the Gallows" and Camus's "Reflections on the Guillotine" together constitute an eloquent appeal for the abolition of capital punishment. Throughout his life, Camus intervened repeatedly in a variety of ways to defend men against the death penalty, motivated simply by a sense of justice and humanity.

These years were darkened for Camus by the rapidly deteriorating situation in his beloved Algeria, where the Arab nationalist revolt that had begun November 1, 1954, had rapidly broadened into a full-scale struggle for independence on behalf of the Muslim population to whose plight Camus himself had sought to direct attention in earlier years. Muslim aspirations, now championed by a group of determined and ruthless revolutionaries, were being bitterly resisted by the European *pied-noir* element to which Camus himself belonged, and his attempts to promote negotiation and discourage the spread of terrorism, torture, and violence succeeded only in alienating all parties. Unable to associate himself with the extremists in either camp, and concerned as well about the safety of his mother and other relatives and friends, he found himself condemned to a helpless onlooker's role, a sterility whose effects can be seen in *The Fall* and other writings of the period.

Paradoxically, it was just at this time of deepening frustration, in October 1957, that the forty-four-year-old Camus was offered the Nobel Prize for Literature "for his important literary works which shed light on the problems today facing the human conscience." Only Rudyard Kipling had received the distinction at the still earlier age of forty-two. Camus's reaction to news of the award was in keeping with his altruism and honesty. He expressed regret that André Malraux had not received the prize in his stead. He telephoned to his mother in Algiers, to whom his work and life had brought a measure of happiness, and now their voices could touch each other, breaking through the silence of the past. And he wrote a letter of thanks to his primary school teacher in Belcourt, Louis Germain, who had recognized his pupil's superior mental gifts and had sustained and guided him in his early years.

In his speech of acceptance at the Swedish Royal Academy on December 10, 1957, Camus spoke of his conception of art and of the role of the artist in our era. More sensational was an exchange that took place during a debate at the University at Stockholm, where Camus was denounced by an Algerian student as an agent of the French repression then being carried out in their common homeland. Camus's reply to the student's interpellations—subsequently summed up as his "mother and justice" declaration—was in essence that he condemned the blind terrorism that was raging in the streets of Algiers; that he believed in justice; but that if terrorism struck his mother or his family, he would defend his mother before he would defend justice.

This statement was later subjected to various ill-intentioned interpretations, as was Camus's subsequent stubborn silence with regard to the war in Algeria. Although he permitted the publication in 1958 of the articles on Algeria collected under the title of *Actuelles III,* his own rejection of an extremist position deprived him of any real influence in what had become a war to the death between the champions of Algerian independence and those of "Algérie française."

The circumstances surrounding Camus's stage adaptation of Dostoyevski's *The Possessed* in 1959 are indirectly connected with his untimely death in the following year. Indeed, it would almost seem as though he had died because of his love for the theater. *The Possessed* was perhaps the most challenging of the works he had undertaken to adapt for the stage at a time when his own creative vein was showing signs of possible exhaustion. His version of the Dostoyevski novel had been highly successful in Paris, holding the boards at the Théâtre Antoine from January to July 1959 and traveling thereafter to Venice and Lausanne, with Camus himself superintending the production and assuring its proper execution.

In November 1959 the author returned to the family home he had purchased in the village of Lourmarin (Vaucluse) in the South of France. His aim was to continue working on a new novel, *Le premier homme* (The first man), inspired by recollections of his early life in Algeria, and a play, *Don Juan*—a personage who had long fascinated Camus, even if he cannot be said to have served as a role model. Camus also wished to be close to the members of his theatrical troupe, who were continuing their tour in Marseilles.

It was while Camus was returning to Paris after the Christmas holidays, on January 4, 1960, that the car driven by his friend Michel Gallimard suddenly went out of control and crashed into the trees along the roadside, instantly killing the forty-six-year-old author but sparing the lives of the vehicle's other occupants. Camus is buried in Lourmarin, and a monolith dedicated to him stands facing the Mediterranean Sea at Tipasa, Algeria, whose ruins he had celebrated in *Nuptials*.

Francine Faure, the mother of their twins, died twenty years later.

Part II

The Novels

Camus is profoundly opposed to all Christianity stands for: first the notions of incarnation, of grace, of redemption, of repentance, and of collective guilt for some sins committed, unbeknown to us. In that sense . . . Camus stands at the opposite pole from Kafka, "the novelist of impossible transcendence": for Kafka, enigmatic signs appear to point to an inhuman and undecipherable order; for Camus, there is no transcendence whatever. The very notion of sin, he avers, is meaningless to him.

—Henri Peyre, "Camus the Pagan"

2

The Stranger: A Study in Black and White

Algerian sunlight, for Albert Camus, is sometimes "so bright that it becomes black and white," and the countryside, at certain hours, glows "black with sun." Meursault, the protagonist of *The Stranger* (1942), before whose sun-dazzled eyes the parched earth and its vacillating forms coagulate in dark brilliance, commits a murder on a North African beach "because of the sun."

The symbolic novel unfolds in Algiers in the 1930s and narrates, in the simplest language, the story of a Frenchman who, in a fit of apparently inexplicable violence, psychologically and physically blinded by the African sun, kills an Arab—an Algerian Muslim—on a deserted beach. The name of the Frenchman is Meursault, an office clerk without ambition for advancement or success, without aspiration to a better life-style either through marriage, promotion, or transfer to a Paris office. Meursault appears perfectly content with his own existence, his own truths, his own trivial pleasures; he lives in his own private world, indifferent to the opinions of others, without regard for social mechanisms. After the crime, condemned to death on the guillotine, he accepts the verdict without reaction or emotion, without anger or contrition. He is a "stranger" among men, a murderer without guilt, condemned to die because a slight difference sets him apart from others.

Meursault relates his story in the first person, beginning with the bald statement: "Today, mother died. Or perhaps yesterday, I don't know." Whether Meursault's mother died today or yesterday is insignificant; whether the Arab's death was accidental or intentional is irrelevant; that Meursault's life will be cut short because he simply is uninterested in defending himself is inconsequential. "It's all the same to me"; "it's not my fault"; "it doesn't matter"—these are the phrases Meursault uses in reference to the events and vicissitudes of daily life. The principal leitmotiv throughout the novel is "it's not important." Nothing is important except what Meursault himself, in his aberrancy, considers meaningful: the pleasures of certain physical sensations; the rejection of sentimentality and social conformity; solitude; and the ultimate discovery that he can spurn the consolation of religion and the illusion of immortality, to take his place among those privileged "brothers" who have lived out their tragic destinies before him.

In the opening scene of *The Stranger,* which is repeatedly recalled in other parts of the novel, Meursault has been notified of his mother's death and betakes himself to the geriatric home where the old lady has resided for several years. Deepening dusk pervades the little white room that serves as a morgue and where the pale corpse lies draped in black.

Instead of staying awake and keeping watch all night, as is customary and traditional even though purposeless, Meursault dozes fitfully while the other watchers sleep soundly, reinforcing his conviction that basically the dead woman was of no importance to any of them. Yet he will later be accounted monstrous for having slept through the vigil, for not having asked to have the coffin opened one last time to look at his mother, for not having shed a single tear, for not knowing his mother's age, for having left the cemetery immediately after the burial, without kneeling in prayer at the grave— trivial details that prove of infinite importance in helping the jury to decide that Meursault's life should not be spared.

After the funeral, Meursault's solitary life remains unchanged. He continues to devote himself to the usual banal activities and diversions of an obscure bachelor whose job fills his week and whose weekends are spent in the company of a girlfriend, Marie Cardona, a typist who used to be employed in his office. Marie would like Meursault to love her and marry her. He apathetically acquiesces to marriage—it's all the same to him—but admits honestly that he doesn't share Marie's feelings of love. A casual encounter with one of his neighbors will, however, soon change the course of his life.

Raymond Sintès, a brutish-looking, ill-famed pimp, involves Meursault in his private dispute with an Arab mistress. At Raymond's request, Meursault composes and writes a letter inviting the young woman to a rendezvous at which she will be cruelly beaten. Again, as earlier in the story, Meursault hears his own blood pounding in his ears—a clear premonition of death. He nevertheless continues his association with Raymond and his friends, one of whom, Masson, invites him to bring Marie to spend a Sunday at his beach house on the outskirts of Algiers.

Outside their apartment house that Sunday morning, Raymond spots a group of Arabs, among them the brother of his ex-mistress, who has been trailing him ever since the affair of the beating. Later, two of the Arabs unexpectedly appear on the beach where Masson, Raymond, and Meursault are strolling under the dazzling noonday sun. Raymond, alert to the impending danger, assigns responsibilities in the event of a clash: he personally will take on his mistress's brother; Masson is to attack the companion; and, should a third Arab appear, Meursault is to assail him. A bloody battle ensues in which Raymond is stabbed in the arm and mouth, after which the Arabs flee.

Later in the day, Raymond, bandaged and armed with a revolver, returns to the beach under the crushing sunlight, Meursault following to keep an eye on him. They reach a freshwater spring hidden behind a huge rock where the two Arabs are reclining. The overexcited Raymond makes as if to shoot his adversary, but Meursault restrains him, pointing out that the Arab has said nothing nor has even drawn his knife. Meursault suggests that Raymond engage him rather in hand-to-hand combat and leave the gun to him in case the second Arab should intervene. But the Arabs, declining engagement, retreat behind the rock. Raymond and Meursault return to Masson's beach house, intending to take the next bus back to town.

At the moment of reentering the beach house, however, Meursault is seized by an inexplicable immobility, weariness, and apathy, accompanied by a feeling of intoxication and mental confusion. Eventually he turns around and retraces his steps along the beach, the veins of his forehead beating relentlessly under the skin. He longs to quench his thirst at the cool spring and bask in the shade of the rock, but when he reaches the spring, he again finds it "occupied" by Raymond's enemy. Meursault knows that he has only to turn around in order to avoid a confrontation, but, behind him, the beach, vibrating under the scorching, pitiless sun, seems to block his retreat and goads him on towards the spring. Meursault takes a step forward; the Arab draws his knife. The blinding sun, the sea, and the salty perspiration from his own brow drop a veil over Meursault's eyes; he becomes disoriented in time and space. His finger involuntarily pulls the trigger of Raymond's revolver, hesitates, then pumps four more bullets into the inert body on the ground.

Under interrogation by the prosecuting attorney and by the court-appointed lawyer assigned to defend him, Meursault (who would prefer to do without a lawyer) is unable to explain away the facts adduced by way of demonstrating his insensitivity. He honestly was unable to mourn the death of his mother. He knows that he did not return to the spring with the intention of killing the Arab, yet he honestly does not know why he did return, armed, to that particular spot, nor why he hesitated after the first shot, nor why he continued shooting once the body had fallen to the ground. He honestly does not believe in God, nor can he later repent in order to be pardoned; and though he is not hard-hearted, he is honestly unable to shed tears before the image of the crucified Christ that is offered by the prison chaplain. Whatever specious arguments his lawyer suggests by way of extenuation are vehemently rejected by Meursault, who becomes a martyr to strict truth. He does not attempt to justify himself in the eyes of his own lawyer, for he sees the futility of his own words; and though he would like to gain the lawyer's sympathy, he is too lethargic to seek it.

Gradually, as he awaits the leisurely course of justice, Meursault's thoughts change from those of a free man to those of a prisoner, keenly aware of the alternation of day and night. His little cell, with its high window against which he strains to view the light and the sea, becomes familiar, desirable. When Marie comes to visit him, he concentrates his hopes on the delicate fabric that covers her shoulders, which he yearns to grasp but from which he is separated by ten meters of space and two gratings that hold visitors and prisoners apart.

Up to the moment of the trial, Meursault feels no sense of guilt. It is only when the attendant of the geriatric home testifies that the accused did not take a last look at his mother and that he had smoked, slept, and drunk coffee in the presence of the corpse, that the indignation in the courtroom makes itself felt and, ironically, for the first time, enables Meursault to understand that he is guilty. His strict honesty in answering the questions put to him by his examiners has effectively worked against him; he now admits to the desire to weep, so conscious is he of the reprobation he has himself aroused. To this desire is counterpoised the scornful laughter in the courtroom at his truthful answer that he did not willfully intend to kill the Arab, that he killed "because of the sun." His simplicity and his innocence are so obvious that they can only result in a verdict of "guilty."

As the trial proceeds, the questioning and haranguing of his lawyer and the prosecuting attorney seem to reduce Meursault himself to a nonentity. They substitute themselves for him so completely that the central character begins to feel himself outside the entire affair and gains the impression that his destiny is being decided without even involving his own person. (In this respect, the British title of the novel, *The Outsider,* is especially appropriate.) Gradually, the suffocating heat in the courtroom and the interminable flow of words—evocative of the heat and prayers at his mother's burial, and premonitory of his own—together with the endless interrogations and the muddled concepts of a trial in which "everything is true and nothing is true," induce the same feelings of mental confusion and dizziness that had affected Meursault on the beach. Once the verdict of guilty is pronounced, Meursault vents his wrath against the prison chaplain, and at last finds peace and refreshment in the perfumes of the night and the earth, the salt sea air that fills his cell, cooling his burning, beating temples. The hated Meursault must die under the blade of the guillotine. The leitmotiv is again heard: it's not important how or when; he is as indifferent to his fate while still alive as he will be when dead. He opens his soul to the tender indifference of mankind in a world devoid of God, recognizes that he has known happiness through the sheer act of living, and hopes only that, in order to be less alone at his execution, there will be many spectators to greet him with cries of derision, so that he may fully live out his role in life and that his fate may be confirmed by a senseless manifestation of hatred.

Although it appeared in wartime, it is important to remember that *The Stranger* is a work of the prewar years and had been completed before the sudden German attack and collapse of French resistance in the spring of 1940. Its somber, sometimes paradoxical tone is the fruit of Camus's youthful ponderings, his rebellious disgust with the complacency and fraudulence of prewar society, but in no sense a reflection of the deeper, more universal tragedies in the midst of which it came before the public.

Three forms of death underpin the story of *The Stranger:* the natural death of an old woman; the homicide of a faceless Arab; and society's irreversible punishment of a basically honest and potentially salvageable criminal. Camus presents each of the three forms both realistically and symbolically, and links all three by means of sharp, smiting images of awful finality.

His dead mother is a victim of that killing force that is old age, which renders men and women feeble and helpless, then strikes to snatch away the very breath of life. No son or daughter, but death alone, is guilty of this crime. Yet an inevitable sense of guilt—although "it's not his fault"—stirs in the son who has been summoned to mourn, and the elements focused on in the mother's funeral scene convey both the bewilderment and the blindness surrounding death. The unexpected switching on of the dazzling electric lights in the morgue momentarily blinds Meursault. This premonitory scene is immediately followed by a description of Meursault himself, scarcely the bereaved son one would expect to meet, seated beside the bier and drinking coffee and smoking. He has, it is true, hesitated before lighting his cigarette, unsure whether it would be appropriate in the presence of the corpse—a hesitation that will be replicated in the pause between the first shot he fired at the Arab and the subsequent four. The accomplishment of both acts, after the moment of indecision, probably bespeaks Meursault's mental conclusion that "it doesn't matter"—a standpoint that precludes contrition and that, in the eyes of the jury that will condemn him, establishes his guilt. Twice will the attendant be called upon in court to tell the story of Meursault's coffee and cigarette; twice will Meursault be asked why he waited between the first and second shots—only to impress the jury, by his answers, with his guilt and thus to justify its capital verdict.

Even before the court scene in *The Stranger,* Camus had given the reader a foretaste of Meursault under judgment, in a description bringing Shakespeare's immortal lines to mind:

> The jury, passing on the prisoner's life,
> May in the sworn twelve have a thief or two
> Guiltier than him they try. (*Measure for Measure,* II, i)

As the elderly inmates of the geriatric home file silently into the morgue to take their seats opposite Meursault and the corpse—and they are now twelve in the room—he sees them momentarily, in a kind of premonition, as sitting in judgment on him. He is unable to see their eyes "set in a nest of wrinkles" (again, symbolic blindness), and their toothless mouths move in incomprehensible murmuring sounds, perhaps an anticipation of the gentle sounds of the sea and the gurgling of the freshwater spring in the murder scene, or of the interminable flow of words during the court trial.

The funeral procession and burial ceremony take place in mid-morning when the hot sun, the main symbol in the novel, already weighs heavily on the little cortege of mourners—a heaviness later to be mirrored in the murder scene, when the unbearable burning sun, in Meursault's mind, will be "the same . . . as the day I buried my mother." The priest who has been summoned to conduct the funeral calls Meursault "my son." Similarly, in the closing pages of the novel, another priest, the prison chaplain, will call Meursault "my son," provoking thereby a burst of nervous anger on the part of the condemned criminal, who refuses to accept identification with this "father" who represents for him a set of arbitrary beliefs shorn of any reality in this life.

At the close of the funeral scene, the reader is struck by certain images that presage the second death in *The Stranger:* the figure of one of the mourners whose bloodred ears stand out under his black hat; bloodred geraniums growing on the graves in the cemetery; the red earth being shoveled over the coffin of the dead woman; and

Meursault's blood, which he hears pounding against his temples—a phenomenon that is frequently invoked by Camus at moments of high tension in his fictional works.

On the morning of the homicide of the faceless Arab, Meursault is once again "struck in the face" by the strong sunlight, just as his face had been flailed by the brightness of the light that flooded the morgue. On the beach, at the appearance of the Arab, Meursault notes that the overheated sand now looks red to him—a premonition of the bloodshed to come—and when Raymond later relinquishes his revolver to Meursault, the latter notices that liquid sun (blood) "spilled over it." Just prior to committing the crime, Meursault feels his head bursting from the "stabs" of sunlight that rise from the "red" sands. The Arab's knife gleams in the sun like a long, fiery sword pointed at the forehead of Meursault, who confuses the piercing pain of the sun with the sharp blade of the knife. Not Meursault, but the sun alone, is guilty of this crime that Meursault seems to have committed in self-defense.

These beach images lead directly to their capital verdict counterpart—the guillotine. Meursault's head will be severed from his body in the name of the French people. Are the French people, then, not guilty of legalized, rationalized murder, "guiltier than him they try?" (cf. *Reflections on the Guillotine*, Part III, below.) The knowledge that the jury wills his death deters Meursault from any form of reconciliation or repentance, since it empties of meaning all conventionalities, including respectful burial of a mother or returning the love of a Maria Cardona.

The Stranger illustrates the deep internal contradictions within society's conventional attitudes, as well as the typical existentialist themes of the emptiness of the universe and the absurdity of human existence. Meursault, a lonely but, one must imagine, clear-sighted man, gives meaning to his life through his personal attitude and private experience. Like Meursault, Camus appears to be saying, contemporary man feels himself to be in an absurd situation because, even while he seeks value and justification for his existence, he discovers that society and events defeat his purpose. His subjective will would like to aspire to a rational universe and a life that takes men into account, but objective realities impel him in the opposite direction. Unable to accept a reality that is so blind to human aspirations, contemporary man falls victim to an "absurd" malaise. Indifferent, a stranger to himself, like Meursault, he can in the extreme case even allow himself to be condemned to death through sheer apathy.[1]

Camus's message, delivered in a unique, sober, black-and-white style, was received by Jean-Paul Sartre with these words:

The turn of his reasoning, the clarity of his ideas, the cut of his expository style and a certain kind of solar, ceremonious, and sad sombreness, all indicate a classic temperament, a man of the Mediterranean.[2]

In a deeper sense, however, the significance of Meursault's experience for people situated in other times and in other places is something each reader must determine from an individual perspective.

3

The Plague: A Holograph

The Plague (1947) is the story of an imaginary calamity in the French North African city of Oran during the 1940s. The principal character is Dr. Bernard Rieux, a highly dedicated physician whose self-effacing, silent, and watchful mother attends to his household needs while his wife, who is ill with consumption, is wasting away in a mountain sanatorium outside Oran. (The autobiographical elements, here and elsewhere in the story, will not escape the reader.) Other characters who interact with Rieux are Raymond Rambert, a journalist; Jean Tarrou, a mysterious, obviously wealthy tourist who lives in a luxury hotel and cultivates the friendship of Oran's Spanish dancers; Father Paneloux, an erudite Jesuit priest; a certain Cottard, an attempted suicide and an obviously antisocial type, who is connected in some way with the killing of an Arab on a beach near Algiers and undergoes various personality changes during the course of the novel; Cottard's neighbor, Joseph Grand, a municipal employee, who spends his free time perfecting the first sentence of a sentimental autobiographical work that so engrosses him he seems to be "a thousand leagues away from the plague."

The onset of the catastrophe becomes apparent in an ever increasing number of dead rats in the homes and streets of Oran, followed soon afterward by manifestations of the disease in human beings, whose violent and painful death, occurring in a relentless crescendo, leads to the declaration of a state of emergency and the sealing off of the city from the rest of the world. Thus begins a period of exile for the entire population of Oran, intensified in some cases by separation from those beloved beings who fortuitously found themselves outside the city walls at the time of the outbreak. The trapped community's suffering is compounded by fear and by the forced suppression of personal feelings by prefectural decree. Not even correspondence is permitted, lest the bacillus be spread through the postal system. Only telegrams of ten words—scarcely adequate to communicate one's feelings of anguish—may be transmitted beyond the city's walls.

Rambert, the journalist, who has been prevented by the plague from leaving the city, persists in futile attempts to obtain a medical certificate from Dr. Rieux that will permit him to return to Paris to the woman he loves. He bitterly rejects Rieux's arguments that one has to think in terms of the laws of the plague, and accuses the physician of not understanding any language except that of reason and abstraction. Rambert's complaints compel Rieux to reflect more deeply on the concept of "abstraction" in the face of the sick and dying patients whom he treats each day. At first emotionally involved with each of them, even to the point of physical and mental exhaustion, Rieux gradually becomes aware of a distracted indifference in his reaction to the innumerable house calls in which he is exposed to the hysterical responses of the stricken families. He has grown tired of showing pity, realizing that pity is useless; but he nevertheless continues his professional efforts unflinchingly.

Rieux's example serves as an inspiration to Jean Tarrou, the mysterious wealthy tourist, who now proposes a plan for the organization of a volunteer medical service. The growing intimacy between the two will later culminate in a significant discussion, which forms the core of the book's philosophical content (see below). Since Rieux does not believe in God, Tarrou now asks, why does he show so much devotion to a higher principle? The physician's answer is that since he does not believe in an all-powerful God who will take care of the sick, he must do so himself, struggling with all his might against death and without raising his eyes from his work to seek help from the stubbornly silent heavens.

Tarrou's own role in the struggle that takes place within the framework of the volunteer medical service becomes increasingly important, although he minimizes the merit of his efforts out of a feeling that he has no alternative but to act. Rieux and Tarrou are in essence fighting side by side to encourage the people of Oran to do something actively in defiance of death, rather than falling to their knees in useless prayer. Joseph Grand, the petty bureaucrat, who has nothing of the hero in his makeup, likewise contributes to the common effort by setting up a sort of secretariat for medical assistance. A deepening sense of fraternity develops among Grand, Rieux, and Tarrou. The latter two even help Grand search for the right words for his obsessive opening sentence, and later sit up with him when he is stricken with pulmonary plague. Thanks to the injection of a new serum still in the experimental phase, Grand miraculously recovers and is proposed by the narrator as the self-effacing hero of the story: an insignificant municipal clerk who works all day and spends his evenings doing volunteer service even as he attempts to perfect a literary phrase.

Father Paneloux, meanwhile, is making an equivalent effort in his own domain by organizing a week of preaching and prayer. A large audience fills the cathedral, but Paneloux's lashing sermons and predictions of indescribable punishment for some unknown crime serve mainly to aggravate the prevailing fear and desperation rather than to inspire courageous action. Subsequently, Tarrou will succeed in drawing Paneloux into the volunteer brigade, where the priest's view of life will undergo considerable change.

The purposeful conduct of Rieux, Tarrou, and Grand in combating the plague contrasts with journalist Rambert's aimless drifting from café to café and his futile trips to the railway station in the hope of finding a way to leave the city. Unable to depart legally, he seeks the help of Cottard, the small-time criminal, whose pockets are filled by his black-market dealings in cheap alcohol and cigarettes, and who rejoices in the plague since it occupies the attention of the police and diverts them from his own trail. Repeatedly thwarted in his attempts to bribe the city guards, Rambert must start over again and again, each time renewing the broken contact with the organization arranging his escape. His motivation is not fear of death, he explains to Rieux—he had in fact fought on the republican side in the Spanish civil war—but a feeling that a man must live and die for what he loves. To this principle, Rieux opposes the assertion that the question posed by the plague is one not of heroism but of honesty—that is, of doing one's job. Rambert confesses that he does not know what his job is, if it is not to love, to which the sympathetic Rieux responds that he has not made the wrong choice.

On the morning following this exchange, Rambert telephones

Rieux to offer his own services in the volunteer corps until his escape can be arranged. Later, he will renounce all ideas of fleeing, to avoid, as he says, "being ashamed of being happy all alone." His ultimate decision, then, is to continue working with Rieux in a struggle that, he now realizes, involves everyone. Rambert also perceives that with each effort to escape the city he actually forgets the woman he loves in his total absorption in the effort to reach her; but that each time his plans are thwarted, the woman again becomes the center of his desires. (This perception may be taken to illustrate the Camusian and existentialist theme of the necessity of applying oneself to the task at hand, and of the futility and evanescence of conventional desires.)

Under his almost superhuman burden, Dr. Rieux's role in ministering to patients is practically reduced to accompanying the soldiers who transport the sick and dying to the improvised hospitals, providing information to families, and exhorting the volunteer brigade not to neglect its own sanitary precautions. Skeptical and mistrustful of contact with one another, the citizens of Oran at the same time feel the need of human warmth and comfort—a dilemma not unlike that posed more recently by acquired immunodeficiency syndrome (AIDS).

The dramatic episode in which Rieux and Paneloux experience the agonizing cries and cruel death of a young child brings into focus the theme of medicine versus religion. "May a priest consult a doctor?" had been the title of one of Paneloux's sermons. From his standpoint, a physician is the enemy of God, since he is struggling against divinely ordained death. Protesting the child's innocence, Rieux reacts with anger to the priest's attempts to convince him of God's grace. Then, however, he takes Paneloux's hand in a gesture connoting that together they will suffer and combat the plague— and not even God, says Rieux, will be able to separate them. The experience of the innocent child's death has made Paneloux less certain of himself and his credo, and he begins preaching in a different tone, basing his sermons on an all-or-nothing principle. When innocence is tortured, he now asserts, a Christian must either lose his faith or accept being tortured also. Soon afterward, Paneloux, stricken with fever and expectorating a red blood clot, dies in utter solitude, the cause of his death being registered as a poignant "doubtful."

Jean Tarrou, who up to now has kept his mysterious identity a secret, now uncovers his past to Dr. Rieux in a late-night conversation, beginning with the dramatic statement that he was already plague-ridden even before coming to Oran.[1] The earlier metaphysical discussion between the two is here broadened to become the existential center of the novel.

Son of a well-known state's attorney, Tarrou at the age of seventeen had seen his father, sitting in the tribunal garbed "like a red owl," pronounce a sentence of capital punishment against a living man standing before the young man's eyes. Horrified, Jean Tarrou left home and, from that day forward, occupied himself with questions of justice, death penalties, and executions. After having first entered politics with a view to combating society, because it accepts the concept of what to him amounts to legal assassination, Tarrou felt himself "plague-ridden" and never at peace with himself. Indirectly, he felt, he himself has subscribed to the deaths of thousands of men by condoning the actions and principles on which society is based. By granting the "red owls" a monopoly on condemning men to death, he was justifying them. Tarrou firmly rejects anything that causes men to die or justifies the fact that man must die. Now he has learned that by doing everything in one's power to combat the plague—to "minimize the damage," as he puts it—one can find, if not peace, at least a good death.

Tarrou sees on this earth only scourges and victims. He will fight at Rieux's side, against the scourge, on the side of the victims. He also perceives a third, limited category: real doctors. They are few and far between, but Tarrou will strive to find his place among them—which means, for him, setting out in search of peace. To Rieux's question whether he knows the right road, Tarrou answers: "Yes, sympathy," by which he seems to mean understanding men as fully as possible. Tarrou's conclusion is that one must exert all efforts to become a saint, even without believing in God: "Whether one can be a saint without God is the only concrete problem that I know today." Rieux's position is slightly different. He rejects any form of heroism or saintliness in order to pursue his single purpose—that of being a man. "We're searching for the same thing," Tarrou acknowledges, "but I am less ambitious [than you]." Their partnership is sealed by a swim in the darkened, velvety sea, in perfectly synchronized strokes that are stunningly described by Camus. After this exchange in the name of friendship, the two men resume their work in combating the relentless plague.

Finally, it is officially announced that the scourge has been conquered, and there are general jubilation and festivities, in which Tarrou, Rambert, and Rieux take part. Only Cottard is dismayed at the routing of a condition that has guaranteed his own safety. In a subsequent dramatic scene, this now-insane criminal fires on the crowd outside his home before his capture by the police.

The inaccessible city having now been opened to the outside world, trains enter the railway station bringing back those who had been waiting beyond the walls, and reuniting Rambert with the woman he loves. Tarrou, however, now has himself contracted the disease. Contrary to regulations that require his isolation, Rieux and his mother nurse Tarrou in their home, spending the entire night at his bedside as parties to his formidable and vividly described struggle against death, all three linked in silent affection. Rieux weeps tears of frustration at the death of his friend, yet he knows he has himself won the game of life that Tarrou has lost. Two complementary concepts—the warmth of life and the image of death—together summarize Rieux's knowledge of the plague, friendship, and tenderness. To remember them one day—to know and to remember—is perhaps what Tarrou meant when he spoke of winning in the struggle against death. Armed with this knowledge, Rieux is able to receive the news of his own wife's death calmly and philosophically.

The plague has now spent itself completely. Terror has ended, but, the reader is told, there is no final victory. Much remains to be done, over and over again, in this absurd world, to combat terror and its insidious, tireless weapons. Rieux, who finally discloses that he himself is the narrator, continues his work against the never-ending diseases that are a part of the human condition. Having sought in vain the meaning of the period of exile and desire for reunion that he has just lived through, his search is now directed toward finding an answer to man's hope. The only practical satisfaction of this question is contained in the words *human tenderness*—not only for the strong and innocent who have died during the scourge, but for all the inhabitants of those "happy cities" where dead rats and the plague bacillus may reappear. Then, says Rieux, human tenderness will take the form of helping victims of the scourge; of reminding others of the violence and injustice being perpetrated against them; of breaking one's silence to say simply that, in the midst of scourges, there are more things in man to admire than to scorn. Not all men can be saints, but they can try to become real doctors—such is the conclusion of *The Plague.*

Like all Camus's writings, *The Plague* is open to varying interpretations. It may be read as an allegory of German occupation and French resistance in World War II, or, more broadly, as a paradigm of man's ability, through individual choice, to mitigate the evils endemic in the human condition.

The novel can also be seen as a symbolic representation of the misery of human existence; as an allegory of war, evil, or thirst for power; as a warning against the horrors of bacteriological warfare; as a call to revolt against mankind's "absurd" metaphysical and historical condition; or as a portrait of any modern city, outside of any specific political or historical context, whose thoughtless, frivolous, venal citizens, oblivious to the deeper sense of nature and love, are prone to enjoy the "simple joys [of life on] Saturday evening and Sunday," dedicating the "rest of the week to making a lot of money." Camus's reason for choosing the Algerian city of Oran for the story's setting is clear from a description in one of his essays: Oran, to him, is a desert place, "without soul and without escape . . . [which] turns its back to the sea," in effect denying nature and its beauty.[2]

Structurally, *The Plague* embodies five graphic parts in a sequence that seems to rise and fall with the statistics on inroads of disease in the stricken city. Indeed, Camus, in the vest of Dr. Rieux, seems to be writing up a formidable patient's chart of a Leviathan—the macrocosm that is Oran—recording fever, pressure, respiration, and mortality data in gigantic graphic form. Mass burials, cremations, and an impersonal, smoothly functioning administration may be read as symbols of the vast bureaucracy of totalitarian states and Nazi death camps. The tempo and dynamics of the disease are explicated in a restrained, deliberate and dry tone by the narrator, who also relates the minutiae of daily life in the plague-ridden city. In the third part of the novel, for example, he comments on the lugubrious mass burials and the city's increasingly somber mood. Although the townspeople continue to live under the illusion that they are acting as free men, in reality the plague has eliminated individual destinies, compelling a wholesale acceptance of standardized thoughts and feelings. The ever-increasing number of patients within the city walls necessitates transforming the sports stadium into an internment camp, where quarantined inmates do nothing, think of nothing, all day long. No longer caring how they dress or eat, the citizens adapt and resign themselves to death and suffering. The plague has destroyed all power to love and keep friendships, for love and friendship require time in the future, whereas only moments of life are left to the citizens of Oran. "The entire city looked like a [public hospital] waiting room," writes Camus (interpretative addition mine).

Some of Camus's most penetrating observations on human emotions and psychological reactions may be found in the pages describing the effects on the soul of the invisible scourge. During the period of separation of couples and families, human sentiments undergo surprising changes: husbands and lovers grow increasingly jealous, the fickle become faithful, the heretofore aloof and indifferent child now attaches himself affectionately to his parent. Repeated deferment of the expectation of reunion, projected at first within six months, then one year, then longer, intensifies the sense of exile among these human beings in crisis, whose plight is beautifully and sensitively described by Camus in the second part of the novel. On the positive side, meanwhile, the very despair of those separated from their loved ones saves them from panic: so distracted and preoccupied are they by the selfishness of their love and the problem of reunion, it appears, that should the plague strike them, they would mercifully be taken unawares.

An added phenomenon, in the face of fear and prefectural decrees, is the breakdown of communication among the citizens of Oran. Only the most conventional phrases are uttered; the language of the marketplace replaces that of the heart, says Camus. For him, real communication leads to commitment to our fellow men, whereas the loss of intimate communication is tantamount to the commencement of death. Gradually the city loses its animated sounds, its colors, its joyfulness. Stores close for lack of imported products; rationing is imposed; sea bathing is forbidden; alcohol is consumed indiscriminately, and, though religious sentiment at first seemed to be on the increase, it is now crowded out by a fervor for living and spending before it becomes too late.

The fifth and last part of the novel, which chronicles the gradual abatement of the plague, offers some deeply sensitive psychological observations on the changing attitudes of the now-apathetic population, which speaks with feigned indifference but entertains latent hope that things will improve. Gradually, smiles appear on the faces of the public, which passes from excitement to depression to optimism as the plague continues to wane. It is only the quasi-mythical Dr. Rieux, knowing and serene, who emerges *whole* from the battle, having remained emotionally resolute and unwavering in tenaciously performing his formidable task of ministering to the Leviathan (cf. also *The Myth of Sisyphus*, Part III, below).

Once again, but more positively than in *The Stranger*, Camus paints man as engaged in a struggle against solitude and death. These two novels, *The Stranger* and *The Plague*, forcefully bring to mind the problematic and enigmatical word—*solitary?* or *solidarity?*—evoked in Camus's short story, "The Artist at Work" (see part V, below). In *The Stranger*, Camus seems to have passed negative judgment on solitude,[3] finding it neither good nor healthy and in the end causing Meursault to be considered strange, a stranger, an outsider, and *guilty*. In *The Plague*, the underpinning for the protagonist's adventure is the community of mankind, and Dr. Rieux, the man and his work having become one, dedicated to the service of humanity, is able to find the fullness of his existence and his *guiltlessness*. The solitary and apathetic Meursault accepts the world as it is, come what may; he lacks that form of human aggressivity linked to the instinct for survival that Erich Fromm characterizes as positive, as contrasted with the negative human aggressivity that is linked to death.

Rieux, on the other hand, vehemently rejecting the stock religious justification of suffering, refuses to accept reality without aggressively trying to change it. He finds his greatness in action—

action that releases him from the absurdity of his condition of helplessness in face of the invisible and insidious plague bacillus. Rather than submit or resign himself, he consciously *acts* to combat the ravaging effects of the plague, and succeeds in arousing others to this form of resistance against evil and terror. His sensitivity in carrying out his task demonstrates not only his determination to fight death but also his unlimited respect for the individuality of each human being's personality and capacities.

4

The Fall: A Self-Portrait

Jean Tarrou, the state's attorney's son, carried the plague within him, and so does Jean-Baptiste Clamence, the protagonist of *The Fall* (1956), a renowned Parisian lawyer turned "judge-penitent" (implying that he both judges and does penance).

Structurally, *The Fall* takes the form of a febrile, five-day-long monologue delivered by Clamence in a smoke-filled bar and along the sunless canals of Amsterdam. The narrator, to judge by his own account, was once a virtuous, happy ego, at whom the concierge smiled each morning and to whom each day brought occasion to defend the humble, the handicapped, and the oppressed. The novel opens with Clamence's polite offer of assistance to another bar patron, apparently a cultivated Frenchman, but one whose face and whose replies remain invisible, behind a curtain of silence. Having interpreted between the Dutch-speaking bartender and his new acquaintance, Clamence sets his glass of gin down next to the latter's and begins his apparently plotless monologue, speaking, in essence, into a void. His initial, well-formulated commentaries and epigrams touch on human atrocities toward other humans, and on certain peculiarities of the French and the Dutch. During the subsequent days, Clamence offers a variety of penetrating, cynical, and incisive observations on life, death, suicide, boredom, debauchery, friendship, family, love, truth, hypocrisy, jealousy, and hard-heartedness. To clarify his outlook, he depicts society as structured in such a way that human beings dispose of each other like the tiny fish in Brazilian rivers, which attack in thousands the body of an inattentive swimmer, each fish taking quick, sharp little nibbles until, in a few moments, there remains only a perfectly scraped skeleton. Clamence then makes a few pronouncements on his own identity, in a

transparent attempt to discover that of his evidently sensitive acquaintance, who, however, continues to remain in the shadows.
Earlier in the story the reader has learned that the two resemble each
other in several ways—both are middle-class bachelors of about the
same age, both know the Scriptures well, and neither has shared his
wealth with the poor. Such clues enable the reader to guess that the
two are in fact but one, just as Dr. Rieux himself turned out to be
the narrator of *The Plague*.

After finishing their gin, the two men leave the bar to stroll, under
fog and drizzle, through the grey labyrinth of Amsterdam's canals.
Comparing them to the concentric circles of Dante's hell, they
presently find themselves in the "last circle," after which the fall is
inevitable. Clamence abruptly leaves his acquaintance near a bridge,
explaining that because of a vow made in the past, he never crosses a
bridge at night.

On the following day Clamence begins relating his personal tale
to the listener, painting a most flattering portrait of himself as a
righteous, justice-seeking lawyer with an instinctive disdain for
judges and a passion for defending the downtrodden. He credits
himself with an impeccable record in the practice of his profession;
discreet and dignified rejection of the distinction of the French
Légion d'Honneur; unfailing courtesy, generosity, and magna-
nimity; flawless altruism and civic-mindedness, together with popu-
larity, intelligence, culture, a healthy physique, athletic prowess, and
sought-after dancing ability. Successful in everything he undertook,
Clamence assures his companion that he had reached the point of
total self-satisfaction, a sense of having been chosen through some
superior decree to be privy to the secrets of life.

On a certain night, however . . . (here Clamence interrupts his
monologue, groping for the sympathy of his silent listener) . . . on
that beautiful night in Paris, after an especially good day, crossing
the Seine by the Pont des Arts, lighting up his "cigarette of satisfaction," Clamence hears a burst of laughter behind him. Turning, he
sees no one, and continues walking; but again he hears the laughter,
this time a little farther away, as though farther down the river. He
stops, transfixed. The laughter grows fainter, coming from somewhere behind him, from nowhere, from the river. At the same time,
he hears his heart pounding fiercely—a premonition of death, such

as has been seen elsewhere in Camus's writings. Finally, the laughter dies out completely. Seized with dizziness and gasping for air, Clamence succeeds in reaching the other end of the bridge. Arriving home, he studies his face in the bathroom mirror, finding that it reflects a "double smile"—the first indication given Clamence, and the reader, that the protagonist is actually wearing a mask. From that night forward, Clamence avoids the quays of the Seine and tries to stop his ears to the sounds of laughter that seem to come from within himself. Later in the story he tells his silent listener that when he finally loses all illusions about himself and is completely immersed in the misery of knowing, "the entire universe began to laugh" around him.

Though Clamence ultimately succeeds in putting the incident out of his mind, he no longer is able to live peacefully with himself and his personal convictions. His mental disarray is matched by a deterioration of his hitherto excellent physical condition and the loss of his invariable good humor. He begins to realize that his customary acts of kindness are performed not out of goodness but condescendingly, for the benefit of his onlookers, and that his gestures of altruism are self-centered, motivated by boredom or desire for distraction. A commonplace traffic accident, in which he feels that he cuts a poor figure in relation to the offender, deflates his pomposity to such a degree that he now begins to laugh at himself, at his own speeches in court and in courting women. But his laugh is not his own; it sounds more like the laughter on the bridge.

Clamence continues his monologue, gratified that his fine words seem to be flying centrifugally off his body and uncovering the naked statue underneath. One night in November, crossing Pont Royal after a rendezvous, he passed a thin young lady dressed in black who seemed to be looking down into the water. The nape of her neck attracted him for an instant, but he continued walking until he heard the sound of a body falling into the river. Clamence stopped short, without turning around, then heard a repeated cry that seemed, just like the laughter, to flow down the river, then fade completely away. Trembling from cold and emotion, Clamence attempted to run, but found that his legs would take him nowhere (as with Meursault's sudden paralysis on the beach). Taking a grip on himself, he realized that he must move quickly to save the young lady who had fallen or jumped into the river; but weakness invaded his body and soul and he could only think to himself: "too late, too far." For the next few days he avoided reading the newspapers; but the haunting image of a drowned body had regularly appeared to him throughout his life and travels—on the English Channel, on the Atlantic Ocean, wherever he finds himself on a body of gray water.

Clamence is now obsessed with the thought of death, and with the ridiculous fear that he may die without having confessed to mankind all the lies that coat the naked statue that is himself. His malaise grows more noticeable each day. Every social or professional compliment becomes unbearable, because it seems to increase the number of lies he is living, intensifying the feeling of suffocation that has invaded his body. In despair that he may never be able to catch up in his confession, and determined to demonstrate to the world that he is a hypocrite and liar, he adopts a line of conduct opposite to what he has followed hitherto. Instead of helping blind people across streets, he jostles them; instead of helping the crippled, he deflates the tires of their cars; he insults manual laborers and slaps nursing mothers. The word *justice* now sends him into fits of anger. He becomes antihumanist, and by draping himself in ridicule, he tries to destroy the flattering reputation he has spent a lifetime to build—to the great surprise and perplexity of public opinion. But the mocking laughter continues, and Clamence decides to leave the society of men in order to take refuge in women's beds, which, he cynically observes, are the havens of criminals and the place where they are usually arrested by the police. The self-caressing Clamence is unsuccessful in lovemaking, however, because for over thirty years he had loved himself exclusively: "I, I, I, is the refrain of my whole life and it could be heard in everything I said."

Gradually, he becomes so horrified with the sins of the flesh that he goes to the opposite extreme and embraces the virtue of chastity. Finally, he turns in desperation to profligate drink and debauchery, as a liberating experience that creates no obligations and at least dims the sound of the haunting laughter. But though his debauchery sometimes appears to stop the laughter altogether, his liver and his fatigue decree an end to his orgies. Clamence realizes that there is no escape, that he must submit and recognize his guilt, that no one is innocent and all are guilty, and that each man testifies to the crimes of all others. His clients having drifted away one by one, he decides to close his Paris office and begins fleeing along what Joseph Conrad would call a "line of shadow." In due course he reaches, ironically, a city of waters—Amsterdam—and it is there that he has begun his new practice.

In the last chapter of *The Fall,* a feverish Clamence relates an allegorical tale about his reign as an elective "Pope" in a North African prison camp, where he was called upon to dispense justice among his fellow prisoners. The Pope's transgressions are so notorious that, in the end, he has to be pardoned and do more penance than any other prisoner. Eventually Clamence's monologue crystallizes around the notion that the laughing *must* stop and he *must* avoid judgment, even though there apparently is no escape from sober self-condemnation. Having condemned ourselves in the first instance, the lawyer in him reasons, our only escape is through the extension of condemnation to all others; and since we cannot judge others without judging ourselves, we must abase ourselves in order to gain the right to judge others. To reverse this order of judge-become-penitent, Clamence explains that he himself has been practicing his new profession of penitent. Accepting his own sentences, he ends up penitent-become-judge. The Amsterdam bar is his professional office where he practices public confession and penance as often as possible. The more roundly he accuses himself, the more he has the right to judge others, and the better does he provoke his listener to judge himself, thus relieving Clamence of some of his own guilt. And, in fact, the unidentified listener in the story now seems to feel less satisfied with himself than five days earlier when the monologue started.

His role of judge-penitent allows Clamence to satisfy his craving to be at once both sinner and judge. Now he can continue his old life-style, loving himself and using others, since the confessing of his guilt allows him to start each day with a lighter heart and to enjoy both his natural inclinations and his repentance. This solution permits him to "reign" each night like a divinity from the highest mountaintop, judging the multitude in the Amsterdam bar below, on whose faces he reads the sadness of human existence and despair at the impossibility of escape. Then, each dawn, the "fall" takes place along the canals of the city of waters, whence a voice is heard crying out, begging the young lady to leap once again into the river so that Jean-Baptiste may have a second chance to save them both. "A second chance? How imprudent! Supposing . . . the young lady took us literally? Then I'd have to save her. Brr . . . ! the water is so cold! But don't worry. Now it's too late; it will always be too late. Fortunately."

Clamence's hypocrisy is saved.

The borrowed name of the lawyer is Jean-Baptiste Clamence, an obvious allusion to Saint John the Baptist, whose *vox clamantis in deserto* (voice crying in the wilderness) is echoed in the judge-penitent's relentless confession—a confession that constitutes the entire content of *The Fall*. Moreover, the confession is carried on in places of desolating aspect, akin to those of the scriptural narration, where locusts and wild honey are replaced, however, by glasses of straight gin. A prophetic figure in his own right and disaffected from his people, Saint John the Baptist, who had been born into an important priestly family, undertook an austere life as prophetic preacher and baptizer in the wilderness because of a "call." His dramatic baptisms inspired willingness on the part of repentants to subject themselves to the purifying flood of divine judgment. Clamence, too, in *The Fall*, accepts the "bitter water of [his] baptism . . . water which lies flat, monotonous and endless . . . [in] an immense holy-water font."

The title of the novel, *The Fall*, must be grasped in relation to its complementary concept—"the rise." Jean-Baptiste Clamence, a man of exorbitant vanity and self-esteem, loves heights in both the physical and moral sense, and loves lording it over those beneath him. His vertiginous fall will plunge him deep into the underground locations he loathes, where he will burrow like a moral mole in the realm of conscience and impotence in search of his true self. The successful and conceited Clamence had soared high above his contemporaries, but the body of the stranger falling from a Parisian bridge into the fast-flowing river has precipitated his own loss of innocence and his own giddying fall.

Just as Meursault killed "because of the sun," Clamence allowed the young lady to die because of the cold. One motive appears to be as rational as the other. But whereas Meursault was too honest to repent just in order to be pardoned, Clamence is too hardened a hypocrite to become a martyr to truth. Clamence, it is true, is but one casual individual, one representative of the entire human condition. But all people, Camus appears to be saying, are faced with the impossiblity of justifying themselves unless they hide behind a mask—a point that is admirably illustrated in the dramatic work of another Nobel Prize winner, Luigi Pirandello, in his collection, *Naked Masks*. People are all condemned eventually to make that ineluctable leap into the river—or into hell. Their deepest desire, the eternal dream of their finite nature, is to abrogate this fate—that is, to achieve immortality by seeking to move up to "high places," from which their exit can only take the form of a fall or a sunless gray exile.

One can see in *The Fall* the figure of a successful but vulnerable writer, such as Camus himself, who is struggling to escape from the heights of the literary establishment in order to find his true self. But the portrait he has so artistically constructed is actually "of everyone and of no-one," in Clamence's words. At first a vague image of a man in a smoke-filled bar, the portrait gradually develops, à la Ingmar Bergman, into the likeness of an individual who, in the course of his verbal and mental strictures, sheds his outer personality until a "naked statue" remains as its irreducible core. Facing himself in the mirror that shows him a "double-faced, charming Janus," he recognizes that not even his mask is so admirable as he thought it was. Moreover, he discerns that the mirror's reflected image is not only of himself but of *all* his contemporaries, all tumbling headlong in the great universal fall from safe places of false refuge.

Camus has made his readers all suspicious and critical of their own apparently good sentiments; he asks them to recognize their good badness and their bad goodness; their sincere falseness and their false sincerity; he shows them how to challenge themselves whenever they begin to feel virtuous. The first title Camus had thought of giving to the novel was "The Cry," an allusion, perhaps, to the voice of Saint John the Baptist. But "The Cry," like "The Fall," is a symbol of our anguish and our revolt against ourselves. Clamence's refusal to heed the cry of the drowning woman demonstrates that a single act of withdrawal from basic human solidarity suffices to cancel any presumption of natural innocence.

In the Sistine Chapel fresco depicting the fall of the damned, men covered with dirt, pulling their hair, lacerating their faces with their nails, await final judgment in the place that Clamence calls the "vestibule of Dante's inferno." It is not necessary, however, to await the Last Judgment, Clamence informs his acquaintance, for "[i]t takes place every day."[1]

A thin but haunting tale, *The Fall*'s full impact will make itself sharply felt if the reader should happen to cross a deserted bridge on a cold, dark night. Suppose *you*—"*hypocrite lecteur, mon semblable, mon frère*," to use Baudelaire's terms—suppose *you* heard a body falling into the water. What would *you* do?

Though conventionally classified as novels, the three book-length works of fiction that have become perhaps the best known of Camus's writings offer three different, yet equally radical, departures from the novel's traditional form and subject matter. All three of them, moreover, are autobiographical at least in form, though the reader is never sure how far Camus is drawing upon his own experience, or expressing his own thoughts and feelings, as he probes the hearts and minds of his protagonists.

The Stranger is the story of a senseless, unmotivated crime, and of the perpetrator's trial and conviction, as recounted by the singularly commonplace and unimaginative individual who committed it. In *The Plague,* the moral and physical ravages of a mysterious pestilence are described by an anonymous narrator, who turns out to be the physician most actively involved in combating the disease. Finally, *The Fall,* a mirror of Europe's postwar disillusionment, takes the form of a prolonged dramatic monologue, in and around a sleazy Amsterdam bar, by an expatriate French attorney who devotes five days to denouncing the depravity of society and his own moral nullity.

What unites these works, aside from the virtuosity with which Camus manipulates their formal attributes, is the importance he attaches to human life, threatened as it is by totalitarianism and terrorism, or by death-inflicting acts of senselessness or negligence. The menace to humanity is symbolized in *The Plague* by an elusive death machine that progressively gives signs of getting out of hand. In *The Stranger* glisten a gun and the blades of a knife and of a guillotine: the Arab stabs with his sharp knife, the Frenchman fires five bullets from his gun, and the state joins in by sliding a heavy blade down two vertical guides to effect a beheading—and none of these three senseless aggressors is *really* intent on killing. In *The Fall,* the negligent Clamence's glimpse of the young lady's nape—exactly where the blade of the guillotine falls—followed by the fall of a body that will die, completes the symbology.

The unifying element of the three novels is also the moral seriousness Camus brings to dissecting the hypocrisies, subterfuges, and evasions of so-called civilized society. With his rejection of Christian theology, Camus combines an insistence on absolute intellectual honesty, adherence to the highest ethical standards, and deep reverence for life. It is true that the positive moral teaching of these novels tends to be somewhat ambiguous: why should one condone a Meursault who killed a faceless Arab or sympathize with a Clamence who allowed an unknown lady to drown? Is it because the victims were unknown to them? Are one's moral responsibilities limited to the circle of one's intimates and acquaintances, or should they encompass all of humankind? Had the victims been known to the protagonists, would they have acted differently under the same circumstances of scorching sun and icy waters, or do extremes of hot and cold, even figuratively, lessen one's moral obligations? Only *The Plague,* in fact, can be read as a study of responsible conduct in the face of calamity. But each of the three novels, in one way or another, compels the reader to examine his own beliefs and attitudes, and to consider how far they coincide with the qualities, good or bad, of Camus's fictional characters.

Part III

The Essays

If Camus had never written any fiction or drama he would still be likely to rank among the outstanding authors of the twentieth century solely as a literary essayist. . . . [The exemplary quality of his prose] is distilled in its purest, most autonomous form in the essays.

—Donald Lazere,
The Unique Creation of Albert Camus

5

The Wrong Side and the Right Side: Chiaroscuro

The five short, occasional essays or sketches published in 1937 under the title *The Wrong Side and the Right Side* (UK title: *Betwixt and Between*) were written when Camus was still in his early twenties. Dedicated to his professor, Jean Grenier, *The Wrong Side and the Right Side* is ranked by some critics among Camus's most moving writings.

The five personalized compositions, entitled "L'Ironie" ("Irony"), "Entre Oui et Non" ("Between Yes and No"), "La Mort dans l'Ame" ("Death in the Soul"), "Amour de Vivre" ("Love of Life"), and "L'Envers et l'Endroit" ("The Wrong Side and the Right Side"), interweave sun and shadow, life and death, almost in the manner of seventeenth-century paintings. Camus's preface (written much later than the essays) is an acknowledgment of his love for humanity and his feelings of solidarity with the entire world; yet it is also a confession of his incapacity to feel humble except before the lives of the poorest or before the great ventures of the human mind. Between the two, he sees a contemporary society that moves him only to derision.

The first essay, "Irony," takes the form of a miniature trilogy or triptych. The reader is first introduced to an energetic young man who has been generously and altruistically devoting himself to a lonely old woman, but who roughly breaks away one evening with a feeling of savage hatred and a desire to slap her because she tries to hold him back from attending a comic film with his friends. The

71

young man's behavior, which leaves the helpless woman in tears and darkness, forcibly reminds the reader of some of Clamence's abject conduct in *The Fall*. A second vignette describes an old man who is no longer listened to in conversation and whose advice is unheeded. He embodies that terrible aspect of old age, the condemnation to silence and solitude. The third and last sketch describes the illness and death, amid the indifference of her family, of an unpardonably tyrannical grandmother (a clearly biographical reference). The three vignettes are painted darkly, for the incongruities of irony are somber, yet Camus steeps them in "all the light of the world," a light whose source is the burning sun that, at least, "warms our bones."

"Between Yes and No" describes a conversation between a sensitive son and his simple, humble mother at that hour of the day that is like an intermission between yes and no, between the time of hope and the time of despair. The few words exchanged between mother and son (who is perhaps a prototype of Meursault in *The Stranger*) are fraught with the simplest lessons of love and poverty. From them the son infers that, between the alternatives of suicide and blind acceptance of life's absurdities, there is also the position of the thinker who rejects suicide and persists in living and in questioning the meaning of life and death, regardless of whether his doubts are answered.

"Death in the Soul" is Camus's story of his brief stay in Prague in 1936—a lugubrious episode that seems to have been characterized by existential feelings of exile, anguish, nausea, and solitude. The culminating horror is his account of the death of the lonely man who occupied the hotel room next to his—horror compounded by the fact that he, Camus, a prisoner of himself and of his despondency, had been shut up in his own room at the time, idly scanning the instructions on a tube of shaving cream and insensitive to the dying man's need for human solidarity. He leaves Prague with the dizziness of one who has gazed too long into a bottomless pit (the underlying theme of *The Fall*). The odor of death and inhumanity that accompanies him during his travels in central Europe is dissipated, however, when he reaches Italy. Sating his vision upon one of the world's most beautiful landscapes, with its cypresses, fig trees, and olive groves bathed in sunlight, he finds the strength to accept courageously his consciousness of life's truths, however crushing.

"Love of life" describes another dimension in the balance of life: a noisy cabaret in Palma de Mallorca is contrasted with the silence and emptiness of the cathedral quarter and a Gothic cloister. The limitless love of life that comes over him as he contemplates this contrast quenches Camus's spiritual thirst for the moment, yet brings the realization that it will inevitably return.

Lastly, in "The Wrong Side and the Right Side," the essay from which the collection takes its title, Camus evaluates two contrasting figures. A strange, lonely old woman who invests in an expensive tomb, and prays there every Sunday afternoon, discovers a scattering of violets left by some sympathetic passersby who have noticed the absence of flowers on All Souls' Day. In the eyes of the world, she realizes, she is already dead. Diametrically opposed to her is a contemplative man who observes and meditates on the sunlight, shadows, and colors in the foliage outside his window. With joy, he allows the god that inhabits nature to caress his senses and reverberate deep within his body and soul. Each of these figures has its acknowledged place in reality. Rather than make a choice between the two, Camus concludes, he will have the courage to keep his eyes open both to death and to light, to paradoxical truths and to the antitheses of life, which he cannot completely grasp but must accept and bring into balance within himself.

The Wrong Side and the Right Side describes the immediate world of Camus's concrete experiences and the lessons he learned as a sensitive boy condemned to poverty and perplexed, at times, by the incomprehensibleness of life.[1] Brooding on the underlying pathos of the human situation, he learned to love life, to express pity and gratitude toward others, to pay tribute to humanity and to simplicity, and to observe the effects on the soul of sunlight and shadow.

The five essays illustrate a phrase from the author's own preface to the collection: "Solitude unites those society separates"—a phrase that overturns the seemingly negative judgment passed on solitude in *The Stranger.* Here, for Camus, the universal feeling of solitude gives rise to a fraternal linkage among men, one that must be combined with kindness of heart and merciful charity. (Such sentiments will be illustrated at greater length in some of the short stories; see part V, below.) A certain measure of solitude is needed in the life of every man, he argues, not only to achieve unity with his fellow men but also to break the mold of routine stability and uniformity into which society presses him. Moments of solitude help men to redefine their sense of self and to put the belief in their own immortality into proper perspective. Solitude also helps man to create a link with eternal, indifferent nature, and to intensify in this way his appreciation for the boundless joys of life.

Basic to Camus's conception of nature and life in *The Wrong Side and the Right Side* is the balanced disposition of light and shade, of positive and negative values. Skillfully manipulating his effects of highlight and shadow to focus upon the various forms of poverty of both body and spirit, Camus implicitly defines his choice of the "right side" in a synthesis that resolves the contradictory elements of light and dark, *chiaro* and *oscuro*. He himself is nothing more than a mortal man (*scuro*, obscure, dark); but he is a man who reaches eternity (*chiaro*, clear, light) at each instant of this absurd life.

6

Nuptials and *Summer:*[1] Panchromatic Sunlight

A sun- and sea-bathed atmosphere of pagan sensuality is everywhere diffused in *Nuptials*, four essays written in 1936–37 and published in 1939, and *Summer*, written between 1939 and 1953 and published in 1954.

The opening lines of the first essay of *Nuptials*, entitled "Nuptials at Tipasa" (a seaside village some forty-five miles east of Algiers), conveys the tone of the entire collection: "In the springtime, Tipasa is inhabited by the gods and the gods speak through the sun and the perfume of absinthe, the silver-clad sea, the raw blue sky, the flower-covered ruins, and the billowing light in the heaps of stone." Camus revels in this manifestation of nature, which attracts and takes possession of him like an Eleusinian votary. Filled with strength and tempered by tenderness, he lies upon and caresses the flat stone slabs of Tipasa's ancient ruins, crushing the scented absinthe beneath him and trying to synchronize the rhythm of his breathing with that of the earth. As this is accomplished, his heart grows calm with certitude and fulfillment.

At Djemila, another archaic North African site that lends its name to the enthralling second essay, "Wind at Djemila," Camus bathes in the violence of sun and wind, actually *becoming* the wind that sweeps through the ancient arches. In still another ceremonial mystery, the wind synchronizes the beating of his blood with nature's heavy, sonorous heartbeat, echoing through Djemila's mountains, while the living face of a horned god in the pediment of an altar looks on.

In "Summer in Algiers," Camus attests his love for all that is lovable in his native city, whose gentleness he elsewhere describes as "rather Italian." Nature here is prodigal, giving of all its splendors, gratuitously, to the poor and to all who will open their hearts and their senses to receive them. In the sea off Algiers's beaches, he feels like a god, a part of nature, and close to all his fellow men through the sheer pleasure of living.

The fourth essay, "The Desert," is a paean to Italy, especially Florence, Fiesole, and Pisa, where Camus's travels in the summer of 1937 revealed to him much that recalled his native Algeria. The sun that shines on Tuscany is the same that shines on Djemila, the breeze in the Boboli gardens is that same deep breathing of the earth that he had heard in Tipasa, and the warm flagstones in the Fiesole cloisters, the deep blue sky and the scent of Tuscan trees and plants, arouse in him the same sensual feelings as in Algeria itself. Struck by the magnificence of the countryside, the beauty of the afternoon sunlight on vineyards and olive groves, and the sensuous grace of the Tuscan cities, Camus enters into blissful harmony with the Italian sun. He finds a kindred soul in Saint Francis of Assisi, lover of poverty, nature, and all living things. Fired by what he calls the three virtues of the Tuscan painters—silence, flame, and immobility— Camus plunges into the delights of Florentine art and undergoes a quasi-purification of his own soul.

Of the eight essays contained in *Summer,* some rank among Camus's most beautiful compositions and are classified by many critics as imaginatively heightened prose poems. "The Minotaur or A Stop at Oran" describes Algeria's second city in unflattering terms as one that turns its back to the sea, and whose inhabitants are bound to be devoured by the monstrous Minotaur. Oran, in this essay, is a dusty, lethargic place, without soul and without resources, where European and Oriental bad taste combine and reinforce each other. A city of boredom and spiritual isolation, Oran was later to be chosen, as has been seen, as the setting for *The Plague.*

The second essay, "The Almond Trees," written in 1940 as World War II was gaining momentum, offers a delicately balanced contrast between war and life. It constitutes a kind of appeal for moral resistance against resignation, renunciation, or abandonment to evil. Camus evokes with poetic sensitivity the white almond blossoms that suddenly burst into bloom in Algiers after a cold, pure February night. In metaphoric language he records his wonderment at the way this fragile blanket, resembling snow, resists the battering wind and rain coming from the sea. In a Europe full of tragedy, Camus often thinks of the almond trees' resistance, made possible by their symbolic whiteness and the sap circulating within their branches.

The third and fourth essays, like "The Almond Trees," are very short. "Prometheus in Hell," which evokes the plight of modern man, offers a preview of the long essay *The Rebel* (see below). "Little Guide to Cities Without a Past" celebrates Algiers, Oran, and Constantine in a slightly humoristic tone, parodying the clichés of a tourist guidebook but again revealing the depth of Camus's love for Algeria.

"Helen's Exile," the fifth essay, poses the problem of the relationship between Christianity and Hellenism, or Greek civilization. Europe, Camus asserts, has exiled beauty from its history and is engaged in the criminal folly of destroying the beauty both of nature and of civilizations. "We light, in an intoxicated sky, whatever suns we want," he writes, alluding to the red glare of rockets, bursting bombs, and projectiles of destruction. Citing the "miserable tragedies" of his contemporaries, he accuses them of turning their backs on nature as though ashamed of its splendor. An outspoken ecologist before the time, Camus inveighs against human as opposed to natural constructs, denouncing those who deliberately amputate and contaminate those parts of the earth that make for its very permanency.

In the sixth essay, "The Enigma," Camus evaluates his own work as an artist in search of his truth and his relationship with his public (see also "The Artist at Work," part V, below). While recognizing that the pessimism of some of his works has caused him to be labeled a writer of despair, he nevertheless affirms that an inexhaustible sun shines in his pages, that he has succeeded in overcoming the "enigma" of his despair, and that his "invincible summer" burns throughout the seasons of anguish and distress.

"Return to Tipasa," the seventh essay of *Summer,* written in 1953, recounts Camus's passionate pilgrimage to the village he had already described in *Nuptials*. After a lapse of years, he finds the sea and the sun of his idealizations unchanged. Reverently he touches the ancient beauties of the Tipasa ruins, hears his heart beat again in their stones, sun and light, and regains sufficient strength to return to what, for him, will always be the dark continent of Europe.

The last essay of *Summer*, entitled "The Sea Up Close," was inspired by Camus's trip to South America in 1949. This essay takes the form of a curious ship's log, supposedly written by an ocean traveler who "weds" the sea. Every aspect and movement of the water is described with a poetic sensuality as though part of a pagan wedding. The ocean's spray is strewn with camellias; off the coast of some vague southern continent, the sea is covered with "strange yellow flowers," and an "invisible song precedes [the ship] for many long hours." The ocean's foam is the "saliva of the gods"; in the ship's wake unfolding patterns create an image of a blue and white cow; under the burning heat of high noon, the sea is personified as an exhausted mistress, scarcely able to lift herself up, lying face down on the ocean's bed; then, pale, as the waves swell and darkness falls, she turns to offer her humid face to her lover. Under the moonlight, a corridor of sea is a rich river of milk flowing into the dark ocean. So absorbed is Camus's narrator in the sea, his "bride," that he scarcely takes notice of the lands lying along the ship's route. Telescoping long distances into four short sentences, he passes the Azores, Cape Horn and the Cape of Good Hope, Vancouver, Easter Island, Desolacion, and the Hebrides. The tone of his description continues ceremonial and symbolic: latitudes wed longitudes and the Pacific drinks the Atlantic. From the ship, the narrator finally describes the coast of South America, but nothing seems to interest him except the experience of swimming for an entire day at a deserted beach and drying in the sun. After this day in physical contact with the sea, he returns to his ship. The calm sea has grown even more peaceful, as though it were his own soul, and he senses that it will be the sea that will ultimately help him to die.

These essays are redolent of Camus's warm personality and of his love for Algiers and its surroundings: the sea, visible from every street corner, or framed by ancient ruins outside the city; a certain weight and color of the sun; the prodigality of nature; the beauty of the North African race. Camus and his fellow Algerians enjoy complete freedom, swimming and running on the beaches, and he achieves complete gratification of the senses as his naked body enters the dialogue between stone and flesh, between the sun and the seasons. The blood in his veins beats with the same pulsations as the sun at high noon, in a rhapsody of sense experiences that fill him with joy at simply being alive.

Nuptials and *Summer* are the two works that best reveal Camus's so-called neopaganism. The Mediterranean light, the array of nature's color spectrum, and the "melody of the earth" that saturate the essays seem to identify their author more closely with ancient paganism than with the value systems of traditional Christianity. Intoxicated by the pleasure of immediate existence, he is too enraptured by the beauty of this planet and his own zest for life to long for or seek salvation in another. Squalid and absurd as human fate and the weight of the world may be, they are nullified in these essays by a total abandonment to the great universal love and compassionate collaboration between man, sun, sea, and the perfumes of nature. In natural splendor and panchromatic sunlight, Camus finds serenity, strength, and the courage to defy injurious destiny.

7

The Myth of Sisyphus: Abstract Expressionism

Sisyphus is the mythological Greek king of Corinth who was condemned to push a heavy stone up a steep hill only to have it roll down again as often as it nears the top. Camus's work, subtitled "Essay on the Absurd," is a modern version of the myth, in which, says the author, one must imagine Sisyphus happy. Why?

The book, dedicated to the editor and fanatic worker, Pascal Pia (see Part I, above), contains four essays: "Un Raisonnement absurde" ("An Absurd Reasoning"), "L'Homme absurde" ("The Absurd Man"), "La Création absurde" ("Absurd Creation") and "Le Mythe de Sisyphe" ("The Myth of Sisyphus"), together with an appendix entitled "L'Espoir et l'absurde dans l'oeuvre de Franz Kafka" ("Hope and the Absurd in the Work of Franz Kafka")—all of which are well summed up in the epigraph from Pindar's third *Pythian Ode:* "O my soul, do not aspire to immortal life, but exhaust the domain of the possible."

Camus disclaims, at the outset of this difficult and involved discussion, any attempt to present a system of metaphysic or a credo. The essay, he asserts, is merely a description of a sickness of the mind (*"un mal de l'esprit"*). The concept of the absurd is taken as a point of departure, rather than the conclusion, of an "absurd philosophy," which, he claims, is unknown in his era.

The first essay opens with the abrupt statement that the only really serious philosophical problem is that of suicide, and that judging whether life is worth living or not is equivalent to answering the basic philosophical question. What is important, he asserts, is the meaning of life—and not death, which one can take or leave, as witness Galileo's decision that scientific truth was not worth defending at the cost of being burned at the stake. The subject of the essay, then, is the relationship between the absurd and suicide, and whether the latter, suicide, solves the problem of the former, the absurd.

Absurdity, for Camus, is something different from the dictionary definition. He defines it, rather, as the divorce between man and life, actor and décor. Absurd is the revolt against bodily death; the denseness and strangeness of life; malaise and nausea in the face of man's inhumanity to man; the inevitable and immeasurable fall that follows a glimpse of the familiar stranger one sees in the mirror. The absurd is also the confrontation between an irrational world and the frantic desire for clarity that stirs in the deepest part of man—the confrontation between the human cry and the unreasonable silence with which it is met. The absurd, then, depends as much on man as on the world, and for the moment it constitutes the only link between them.

Camus sees the three elements—the irrational, human nostalgia, and the absurd—as characters in a drama that originates in their contact with each other and ends, necessarily, "with all the logic of which an existence is capable." A cohesive philosophical principle, then, is revolt, i.e., the perpetual confrontation between man and the darkness surrounding him, and his ceaseless demand for an impossible "transparency." Man's consciousness of the ultimate futility and defeat of his task, and his ever-renewed revolt in the face of this knowledge, constitute his refusal to renounce the Sisyphean labor. The absurd man is witness to a universe of contrasts, in which nothing is possible but all is posited, and beyond this—nothingness. He can yield to the nothingness or he can decide to live in this universe and draw his strength from it, refusing to hope, entertaining only indifference toward the future, and cultivating a passion for exhaustion of everything the world has to offer. The three consequences, Camus asserts, I may draw from the absurd are: *my* revolt; *my* freedom; and *my* passion. Through my consciousness I change the invitation to death into a rule of life, and I refuse suicide.

In the second and third essays, "The Absurd Man" and "Absurd

Creation," Camus elaborates on this theme. He focuses first on the figure of Don Juan, who goes from one woman to another not because he knows he can never find a unique and total love, but because he loves each woman with equal enthusiasm and involves himself passionately with all of them. Since Don Juan is a creative being, one cannot imagine him sad, says Camus. Maintaining that creativity alone testifies to man's dignity and gives form to one's destiny, Camus illustrates other creative types. The actor is the absurd man par excellence: he has three hours in which to play roles that live and die on the stage, after which they again become nothing. The actor's vocation, then, is to apply himself with all his heart in order to become nothing at all (like Sisyphus and the fruit of his efforts). Together with Nietzsche, Camus maintains that what is important is not eternal life but eternal animation.

Conquerors, too, know that action in itself is useless, for the only useful action would be to remake the earth and all the men inhabiting it. (Camus knows that he can never remake men, but he acts "as though" he could.) In the past, the conquering of vast geographical distances made for greatness; now, the modern hero must perform his absurd task in his own native land, which is the human being, protesting and sacrificing, alongside with other strugglers, without entertaining hopes for the future. This tenacious revolt against the human condition and this perseverence in the apparently sterile Sisyphean effort require sustained daily effort, self-control, and a precise evaluation and appreciation of existential freedom, just as was true in the case of the conqueror.

The creative person—artist or writer—similarly goes from one description to the next, starting his work over and over again, proposing it as a demonstration of the dead end into which we are all headed. Yet, in the face of this absurdity, the creative person remains serene and persists in loving life. By applying oneself to the maximum, one may achieve only a creation of utter uselessness, but the task has at least given form to one's individual destiny.

The last essay, "The Myth of Sisyphus," presents Sisyphus as the absurd hero because of his passion, his torment, his scorn of the gods, his hatred of death, and his love of life. Sisyphus is superior to his destiny; he is stronger than the stone he is forced to push. The lesson he gives is one of a higher faith, which denies the gods and raises heavy stones. From his vantage point, Sisyphus judges that in truth all is well: a universe without a master does not seem to him either sterile or futile. Each particle of the stone, for him, is a world unto itself. His struggle to reach the top of the hill suffices to fill his heart. And that it is why one must imagine Sisyphus happy.

As with Camus's novel *The Stranger,* the reader is here confronted with what is in essence a work of the author's youth, begun before the war and redolent of Camus's musings of the 1930s, even though its appearance in 1942 took place at a time when the whole basis of Western civilization seemed to have been called in question by the military and political successes of Nazi Germany. This chronological lag is helpful in understanding Camus's apparent obsession with philosophical abstractions and moral dilemmas that seem curiously unrelated to the more contemporaneous issues of war, collaboration, and resistance.

If *The Stranger* remains one symbol of our times, Sisyphus is no less a contrasting symbol. He is the man who knows how to look at himself and at the kingdom of the absurd, squarely and pitilessly, convinced that no illusion of eternity is any longer tenable. The ineluctable absurd can give rise to despair, which could lead man to thoughts of suicide; but it is precisely with the rejection of suicide that Camus begins his essay. For him, suicide is a renunciation and a defeat. What strikes him is not the fact that Sisyphus is a condemned man in a trap, but rather the extraordinary flexibility that characterizes him and the incredible disinterest he can display—disinterest in everything except life itself. This is the positive ethic of the absurd: life can be lived all the better the less sense it has.

Camus's absurd man, alienated by society somewhere between the top of a steep hill and the deep valley below, discovers that life has no transcendent meaning. Yet he infuses his existence with a unique and irreplaceable value by choosing a task that will require futile and even hopeless efforts, given the transience of human endeavors. Each person today may feel himself spiritually crushed under a burdensome stone, anguished by what seems the lack of a preordained purpose or a moral value system. To counteract one's feelings of frustration and futility, Camus recommends a personal revolt and a determination to succeed. By declining any invitation to the easy way out, by persisting in one's heroic, monumental, though hopeless tasks, by prolonging and savoring every moment of life, one can revolt against the unknowns of an irrational world. One must maintain constant lucidity and reject despair, even in the knowledge that after one has played one's role, nothing remains.

Man must never tire of pushing the stone up the hill. He must will to construct his elusive and unknowable happiness. As soon as the stone tumbles down, he must return to the task. The moment of defeat is there, but to start the useless labor again is to achieve superiority over a fixed destiny. Relentless torment is the price to be paid for the passion of living.

Why does man/Sisyphus accept this torment if he does not believe in any metaphysic, any higher reality? When asked this question by an interviewer during rehearsals in Milan for his adaptation of Dino Buzzati's *A Clinical Case,* Camus gave an expressionistic reply, reminiscent of the "inner necessity" of the abstract artist, Wassily Kandinsky: "Man perhaps doesn't know what good is, but he does know what evil is, and he knows that to refuse it is possible, and that perhaps it's the only thing he can do. For this reason, Sisyphus starts all over again."[1] Published during the dark years of World War II when the temptation to despair was at its strongest, *The Myth of Sisyphus* tells us something of the grim determination that enabled so many men and women in the occupied countries to risk their lives in what may at the time have seemed a futile gesture.

8

Letters to a German Friend: Miniatures

Together with Vercors's *The Silence of the Sea*, Camus's *Letters to a German Friend* (1945) typify the so-called resistance literature of World War II. Filled with bitter resentment yet ennobled by a sense of objectivity, fairness, and justness, the four letters are addressed by a Frenchman (Camus himself) to an imaginary German during two years (1943–44) of a war in which the two former friends find themselves in enemy camps. The dominant mood of the Frenchman is determination to understand both sides, and he specifies that when he uses the word *vous* in a bitter tone, he means not *Germans* but *Nazis,* and when he writes *nous,* he does not always mean *we French,* but *we free Europeans.* What he reproaches the Nazis for, in abstract terms, is their renunciation of man's struggle against the heavens (the gods) in order to vent their wrath against the earth (men).[1] The opposition presented in the letters is one between two philosophical attitudes, not merely between two nations that happen to be enemies at a given historical moment.

In the first letter, Camus reasons with his German friend along these lines: We Frenchmen, to whom ten centuries of history have given a sense of nobility, have had to resist the temptation to become efficient, instinctive, heroic, and scornful of intelligence like you Germans. France entered the war with clean hands and will come out of it the same way, because she knows that the union of spirit and sword leads to final victory against injustice. Germany's sword, drawn for the sake of the sword and not the spirit, will lose, because truth triumphs over the lie. Germans who love their country love it with a love that is blind, and that is why, predicts the writer, they will lose this war.

In the second letter, in response to his imaginary correspondent's brushing off of the word *intelligence,* the Frenchman dwells on the importance of this word, which infuses him with the strength to gain his victory. The conversational tone continues: You say that French intellectuals, rather than loving their country, prefer despair or chasing after an improbable truth, whereas you Germans put Germany ahead of truth and beyond despair. I answer that if we prefer justice to our country, it is only because we want to love our country in justice, in truth, and in hope. What is truth? I can say only that we know what a lie is. What is spirit? We know only that its opposite is murder. What is a man? Man is the force that counterbalances tyrants and gods. Intelligence requires a large dose of lucidity, which Germans do not have, and therefore they will lose out against the French.

The third letter is dedicated to the defense of an ideal and a hope: Europe. The Germans have given a revolting meaning to the notion of Europe by creating a slave European army, considering Europe a piece of property that produces soldiers, wheat, and inhabitants with regulated minds. For Frenchmen, however, Europe is a land of the spirit, of free intellect, and of courage, where for twenty centuries the astonishing venture of the human mind has been unfolding. Once Germany is defeated, Europe will still be Europe, balanced between the need for sacrifice and a zest for happiness, between the indomitable spirit and the mighty sword.

In the last letter, the Frenchman muses that though he and his friend now are enemies, before the war they had been so similar: both had been frustrated at the thought that this world had no superior logic. But now the two have drawn different conclusions. The German reasons that good and evil are equivalents, to be defined as one will, and that in the absence of human and divine morality, the only values that remain are violence and ruse. The Frenchman, in contrast, proffers no other arguments than a violent taste for justice and a refusal to despair of the human condition, as his friend had done.

The letter closes with an unmitigated condemnation of the German friend, whose logic is as criminal as his heart and who is already dead in Camus's eyes. After the war, however, at the time of judgment, the Frenchman will remember that they both were shaped in the same mold of solitude, caught up in the tragedy of human intelligence. Despite the necessity of having to destroy the enemy without pity, the French will respect their common humanity and refrain from hatred; for though Germany's power must be destroyed, her soul must not be mutilated. "And now I can say goodbye to you," ends the last letter of this monologue-confession to an unknown German friend, which resembles somewhat the technique Camus would later use in writing *The Fall.*

Since, in subsequent editions of the *Letters,* Camus never modified or retracted any part of the text as he had written it, they must clearly be read as an appeal for continuing struggle against violence, not merely as an emotional outburst against the German occupiers. Nor need the reader attempt to attenuate Camus's arguments by citing the rich heritage of German culture. It was the betrayal of this heritage by Hitler's hordes that inspired Camus's most bitter denunciation.

As a political statement, the letters have lost some of their force in view of the present-day closeness of Franco-German relations. But they can still be read as an eloquent refutation of the blind mystique of an all-powerful state, and the vindication of a system of human values for which Camus felt it is worth living, fighting, and dying. Out of the war and the resistance, which brought into close association men and women from all walks of life and different religions and political loyalties, there had grown a deep need for human solidarity, which Camus saw in terms of a united struggle against the common enemy: *destiny.* He sought a solidarity between men that, even if it cannot suppress absurdity, can at least surmount it, as illustrated in *The Myth of Sisyphus* and again in *The Plague.* In the common fight against a scourge, be it political or bacterial, men become linked to each other and gain the solidarity necessary to defy the silent gods.

A moving and meaningful human document in the gallery of Camus's productions, the *Letters to a German Friend* may be seen as miniatures—a word deriving from the Latin, *miniare,* meaning to color with red lead or minium. Both bullets and paint pigments may be made of lead, and the color red may be applied both to blood and to art.

9

The Rebel: A Mural Painting

The Rebel (1951) marks a watershed in Camus's life and literary output. Primarily through its vigorous critique of Soviet Communism, it fueled the dispute with Jean-Paul Sartre that ended in the breaking of their friendship (see Part I, above).

The three important themes contained in *The Rebel* are that of revolt (by revolting, man escapes his solitude and discovers the values that link him to all other men); that of murder (if murder is not justified by society, then that part of man that transcends history will be saved; but if murder *is* justified, only slavery and terror will prevail);[1] and that of solidarity in the struggle against death—in other words of vindicating the meaning of life, since a rebel does not ask for life but rather for the reasons of life.

Camus's introduction is perhaps the part of the book that should be read most carefully, since it illustrates his transition from the phase of the "absurd man," as seen in *The Myth of Sisyphus,* to that of the "man in revolt." In these opening pages, the author proposes to accept once more what he calls the reality of the moment, which he equates with the logical crime, and to examine its justifications. Since every action today results in direct or indirect murder, he asserts, one cannot act before one knows if and why one is causing someone's death. Whereas in periods of nihilism it was useful to ponder the question of suicide, in this era of ideologies one must come to terms with the problem of murder. If, in this era, it has come to be readily accepted that murder may have its justifications, this is because of people's nihilistic indifference toward life. The concept of the absurd, as a rule of life, does not provide one with the values necessary to decide whether a murder is legitimate. Camus cries out that he believes in nothing, and that all is absurd; yet he cannot doubt his own cry, and must believe in his protest, which takes the form of an individual, personalized revolt. In this, man is unique: he is the only creature who seeks to transform himself, refusing to remain what he is.

The body of the long essay traces successively what is called "metaphysical revolt," a study of different philosophical attitudes over the past 150 years; historical revolt, from Spartacus to modern times; irrational state terrorism, as typified by Hitler's and Mussolini's regimes; and what is called rational state terrorism, as embodied in Marxism and Leninism. The essay opens with the direct question: "What is a rebel?" and Camus's striking answer: "It is a man who says no." A slave who has been receiving orders all his life, Camus explains, suddenly finds a new command unacceptable and says no; at the same time, however, he says yes, because in refusing he is acting sweepingly on behalf of all existences at all times, i.e., the community of mankind that embraces all men, including the master who insults and oppresses him. Without this underpinning of solidarity, one cannot speak of a rebel (whose conscience must be that of all mankind), but only of a murderer. Paraphrasing Descartes's "I think, therefore I am," Camus pronounces his famous phrase: "I rebel, therefore we are." To this "we are," he later adds: "alone."

That the slave's revolt represents a good common to all humanity is a concept at variance with most of the historic philosophies of Camus's time, some of which had proved useful in justifying dictatorships born of revolution. Camus thus stood relatively alone, inveighing against any form of servility—individual, political, or cultural—and destroying a good number of leftist myths in the process. In the end, he synthesized his politico-philosophical thought in a lyrical opposition between Mediterranean "balance" and European totalitarianism, closing *The Rebel* on a sort of hymn to the beauty of the universe.

In a more general sense, *The Rebel* marked a new stage in Camus's intellectual evolution, away from leftist militancy and toward a simpler, more profound commitment to pure humanism. In a period when the word *revolution* was much in vogue in intellectual circles, Camus chose rather to center his long and closely reasoned essay on the idea of *revolt,* a concept that to him denoted a spontaneity and naturalness at variance with the suffocatingly antihuman tendencies of organized revolution. In a critical review of the revolutions of the nineteenth and twentieth centuries, and of the philosophies and literatures that sparked them, Camus concluded that these revolutions uniformly culminated in the reinforcement of state power and in increased justification of murder, by which he evidently means political execution. Denouncing the cult of revolutionary violence and the destruction and nihilism it implies, Camus contends that it is not a historical necessity as its partisans allege, and that revolutionaries in fact are guilty of nothing less than legitimized murder. For Camus, concentration camps, misery, lies, and atomic bombs are negations of history and progress: life alone measures the progressive development of mankind. He wonders how man, in the name of revolt, has grown to feel so comfortable in crime, and how human pride has become so perverted as to produce the police states and concentration camps of the twentieth century.

Though Camus's broadly scaled mural is not free of obscurity and ambiguity, there can no be mistaking his dedication to moving mankind away from killing and subjugation in the name of historical revolutions; to invoking a solidarity that will permit man to rise above the contradictions in human relations; and to encouraging the creativity and the transformation implied in his concept of revolt, as a means to a certain aesthetic and ethical perspective for our times.[2] Religions and ideologies of the past, he feels, have crushed men and taken away their liberties. Camus's rebel, moderate yet rigorous, nonviolent yet apparently conceding that murder may sometimes be justified, as in *The Just Assassins* (see part IV, below), helps to keep people from despairing in the face of politico-historical evils and allows people to hope that a better category of men, guided by intellect and humanism, will help destroy nihilism and bring into sight a less mechanized, more humane future. Revolt with moderation implies ordering the disorders of history, Camus tells us. All people carry within themselves their life imprisonment, their crimes, their ravages. Their duty is not to unleash them in the world but rather to combat them in themselves and in others. Revolt, the age-old will not to submit, still today is the beginning of this combat.

Camus's thought in *The Rebel* has been echoed in a phrase by another Nobel Prize winner (1987), Joseph Brodsky, who perceives people living in a totalitarian state as considering their system as good as another and, in the end, regarding it as legitimate. "There is nothing worse," concludes Brodsky, "than a contented slave."[3]

10

Reflections on the Guillotine: A Surrealist Incongruity

Reflections on Capital Punishment, which appeared in 1957, was written jointly by Camus and Arthur Koestler, the Hungarian-born writer contributing the section on death by hanging and Camus the one on death by guillotine. The volume offers an impressive denunciation of capital punishment, conceived as a form of legalized, rationalized murder by an absolutist state.[1] The two authors forcefully enunciate, in their own persons, their aversion for the death penalty—an aversion shared, in Camus's case, by a strange bedfellow who has been described at length in *The Rebel.* This is none other than the notorious Marquis de Sade, whose name survives in the word *sadism* but who actually suffered greatly at the sight of the executions he witnessed from the Bastille, where he was imprisoned during the French Revolution. Sade, Camus explained in the earlier essay, could understand killing in the heat of passion, but executions, after calm and serious meditation and under pretext of honorable discharge of duty, were incomprehensible to him. Sade's hatred of the death penalty was above all a hatred of the men who thought themselves, or their cause, so virtuous that they dared to inflict punishment with finality, when they themselves were criminals.

Camus begins his renewed reflections, not without several horrifying descriptions of beheadings, with the observation that a murderer does not fear death before committing his crime. Since it is only *after* judgment that he fears it, Camus reasons, capital punishment

regarded as a deterrent to crime. Statistics show, more-
~~at~~ capital punishment has not reduced crimes in those coun-
~~where~~ it exists. Laws, to serve as effective deterrents to crime,
~~would~~ have to be so severe that they would not admit extenuating
circumstances and would deny the criminal even a glimmer of hope.
What legislator, asks Camus, would permit such laws to be enacted?

Camus attributes much importance to the fact that nowadays the
state does not publicize executions. They are carried out in secret, he
says, not only because the state cannot affirm that capital punishment serves as a deterrent, but also because it is uncertain of its own
position in killing a man. Is it for the crime he has committed, or for
all the other crimes that could have been committed and were not?
Capital punishment, for Camus, is really a form of vengeance, for it
is a punishment that sanctions crime without preventing it. Since,
moreover, premeditated crime is generally considered worse than
violent crime, the state is guilty of the greater transgression in
carrying out its executions.

Every society contains within itself the criminals it deserves,
Camus further maintains. Citing the deep social problems, especially poverty and alcoholism, that explain the French crime rate,
he exhorts people to condemn the creator of these problems (society) before they condemn the criminal.

Camus then proceeds to dwell upon the irreversibility of the death
penalty, both in the case of the innocent victim and in that of the
salvageable criminal. The state must not execute irremediably, he
maintains; it must always leave a margin for the correction of error
and for the possibility of restitution by the condemned person. Since
no man bears absolute responsibility, no man can be condemned to
absolute punishment. Only in the case of a proven "monster" can
capital punishment be deemed legitimate.

Also to be taken into consideration are the circumstances that
surround the death sentence: the place, differences in juries, or the
skill of a lawyer (cf. *The Stranger*). Times and customs change; he
who is considered guilty today may be judged innocent tomorrow.
Capital punishment, moreover, destroys the only indisputable form
of human solidarity, the struggle against death. Accordingly, it can
be legitimized only by a truth or a principle that stands over and
above men. That is why supreme punishment historically had been
inflicted by religious authorities, in the name of kings as representa-

tives of God on earth. The death penalty could then be viewed as powerful means of procuring the salvation of even the most hardened criminals, who usually repented and confessed before dying. The executioner, in these cases, was invested with a sacred function: that of destroying the body in order to hand the soul over to an unprejudiced divine judgment. Today this reasoning is no longer realistic, Camus affirms. Many judges are atheists, and the assertion that a man must be cut out of society because he is absolutely bad implies that society is absolutely good—a contention that twentieth-century man, as witness to the state crimes of his era, would be quick to deny. State crimes, Camus asserts, have increased infinitely more rapidly than individual crimes over the past thirty years, and the number of common criminals has decreased in proportion to the increase in the number of political criminals. Hence, he claims, it is not unimaginable that any one of us today could be condemned in our state for political reasons. The time has come to stop this progression and to declare that the human being stands above the state.

Camus's eloquent conclusion is threefold. In the united Europe of tomorrow, he asserts, abolition of the death penalty should be the first article in the European code to which all men of good will aspire. If Europe does not see fit to abolish this cruel barbarism, at least the mode of administration should be reformed—in other words, the use of anesthesia should be substituted for the present obscene exhibitionism. There can be no durable peace in the hearts of individuals and societies until death is outlawed.

Camus's words speak forcefully for themselves and call for no additional analysis or interpretation. All arguments in favor of the death penalty seem to pale before the conviction and eloquence of the two authors. As a humanist, Camus hated death, the dark image of the human condition beyond which shines the beauty of human beings united in their struggles for the preservation of life (cf. *The Plague*). He sees in the death penalty all the incongruities and inconsistencies of human behavior. To them he opposes the positive, even surrealistic intention of creating a new, authentic vision of life by releasing man's dormant sensibilities.

The variety of form, content, and mood that characterizes Camus's literary output is nowhere more strikingly apparent than in the

ıve been discussed in the preceding pages. Spanning
e entire course of their author's adult life, they range
fest, most evanescent of poetic sketches to the densely
guments of the two book-length works, *The Myth of
Sisyphus* and *The Rebel*. From an initial childlike exultation in the
beauty of the world, and of life, Camus leads the reader through
grim reflections on the meaninglessness, the "absurdity," of human
existence, inviting him in the end to share his stoical resolve to make
the best of things in unremitting struggle against the cruelty and evil
surrounding humankind.

Three of the volumes of collected essays, *The Wrong Side and the
Right Side, Nuptials,* and *Summer,* are made up primarily of impressions dating from Camus's early years in Algeria, either as
experienced directly or as subsequently recollected. *The Myth of
Sisyphus* records his struggle with the notion of the "absurd" and
his dismissal of suicide as an answer to the silence of the universe. In
his wartime *Letters to a German Friend,* he again rejects despair
and reaffirms his commitment to combat the evils of existence—the
same commitment that will animate Dr. Rieux and his associates in
their struggle against the plague. *The Rebel,* Camus's longest and
perhaps his most difficult work, affirms the right of individual
resistance (or "rebellion") against injustice, at the same time rejecting totalitarian solutions of either the Right or the Left. Finally,
Reflections on the Guillotine argues eloquently against what to
Camus is the "crime" of capital punishment.

Certain common themes run through these essays, for all their
diversity. Frank enjoyment of nature's gifts, sympathy for the downtrodden and disinherited, and hatred of cruelty and oppression are
the determinants of Camus's work, as they were of his life. At the
same time, the transcendental in all its forms is resolutely excluded.
Mankind, for Camus, is alone in the universe, to enjoy its gifts or
suffer its blows without hope of outside assistance or support.
Instead of yielding to despair or pinning one's hopes on miracles,
Camus says, one would be well advised to accept the inevitable and
get on with the struggle.

Part IV

The Plays

[Camus's] natural Mediterranean flair for drama and mystification found an outlet in his passion for the theater—all facets of the theater. . . . A feeling of the stage, of the voice speaking directly to an audience, of dialogue projected across footlights to link audience and actor is present everywhere in his work. . . . [T]here is always a dialogue . . . between himself and his main characters; between them and the reader; between the reader and the author. He and his characters address themselves to an audience.

—Germaine Brée, in her introduction to *Camus: A Collection of Critical Essays*

11

Caligula: Dadaism

Gaius Caesar Augustus Germanicus, nicknamed "Caligula" (from the Latin *caliga*, boot, + diminutive suffix) after the army-type boots he wore as a small boy, became Roman emperor at the age of twenty-five in A.D. 37. At first a gentle and enlightened ruler, after a grave illness he became a megalomaniac and bloodthirsty tyrant. Camus based his four-act play, *Caligula* (1944), on the history of this first in the series of absolute and unbridled Roman dictatorships, in which he found an analogy to the political developments of his own times.

In the first act, the Roman patricians express their concern about the disappearance of Caligula after the death of his beloved sister and mistress, Drusilla. The empire can ill support a period of national mourning over an incestuous love, they comment. Caligula eventually reappears after three days' absence, dirty, distraught, and determined, in defiance of the stupidity and cruelty of the gods who had willed Drusilla's death, to take destiny into his own hands. He now feels the need for "the impossible," he declares. He must have the moon, the only thing he does not yet possess. Drusilla's death has made him privy to the truth that "men die and are not happy." This revelation, the audience is given to understand, is to be the source of the strange and revolting behavior to be witnessed during the remainder of the drama and of Caligula's life.

The devoted and faithful poet, Scipio, insists upon his love for the emperor whose sensitivity and poetic ideals he used to share; but he laments that Caligula, who in the past had sought to become a just man, one who assuages his sorrows through religion, nature, art, and love, now, by his bizarre conduct, is negating the laws of beauty and organization. The first action of this "new" Caligula has been a

101

decree that all patricians must disinherit their families and bequeath their fortunes to the state in order to solve its financial problems. Having accomplished this step, they will be put to death by Caligula's command, for "if the treasury has importance, then human life does not." Declaring that his freedom to act in achieving the impossible will henceforth be subject to no limits, Caligula expresses his hatred and scorn for those who neither crave nor require a similar freedom. Forlornly, he describes to Caesonia, his old mistress, the bitterness of the constant taste of blood, death, and fever in his mouth.

Caligula's ambition, he lets it be known, is to exert his influence over the order of this world. His aim is not simply to equal the gods, but to stand above them. He will be king in a kingdom of the impossible; he will give to his century the gift of equality; and, once he obtains the moon, men will no longer die and they will indeed be happy. The act closes with the cynical, demented emperor calling in the first of the victims whom he has peremptorily condemned to death.

The second act finds the patricians plotting the death of the emperor who has ridiculed and humiliated them and made prostitutes of their wives. Cherea, in this instance, is the rebel who says no, sets about organizing an assassination attempt, and proposes that Caligula be allowed to continue in his madness until he becomes supreme monarch in an empire of the dead. Caligula now enters and provides a frightening demonstration of his freedom to act at the expense of others. He forces Lepidus, whose son he has had killed, to laugh at his stories about another son who is to be killed; he possesses Mucius's wife almost under the latter's eyes; he orders a famine to be engineered by closing the public granaries; he signs new decrees for the execution of some of those who must die for the crime of being Caligula's subjects—a crime of which, of course, all are guilty. The act ends with the maniacal Caligula vaunting his intelligence in hatred, his purity in evil, and his scorn for mankind, in which, he says, he takes "silent refuge."

Act 3 finds the mad emperor, grotesquely disguised as Venus, appearing before the people to receive their offerings. The patricians are forced to prostrate themselves and adore him. Scipio accuses him of blasphemy and of defiling the heavens, now that he has already covered the earth with blood; but Caligula, defending himself, declares that he has now discovered how to equal the gods: it suffices to be as cruel as they are. Scipio predicts the day when legions of "god-men" will rise up against him, drowning his divinity in blood; but Caligula rudely dismisses him on the pretext of having his toenails painted.

Helicon, another courtier, attempts to warn the emperor that the patricians are plotting against his life. Instead of paying attention, Caligula muses, in highly poetic language, over his erotic possession of the moon. Insisting that Helicon bring him the moon promptly, he delivers a long monologue in which he follows out his logic to its final senselessness. Calling in Cherea, the leader of the conspirators, he personally burns the tablets on which the plot is outlined, thus freeing Cherea from guilt and demonstrating his own power to render the guilty innocent—though not, in the long run, to save his own life.

The last act finds the patricians convened in the palace, expecting to be killed en masse but treated instead to a dance by Caligula in ballerina costume. One by one, however, the patricians are in fact led to their death as the emperor, described by Caesonia as "not a sick man but one whose soul is covered with ulcers," officially consecrates the day to art and poetry. Convoking all his poets, he next demands that they deliver extemporaneously recitations on the subject of death. Caligula personally opens the ceremonies by declaring that he recites his death poem every day and that he is the only true artist in Rome, the only one who harmonizes his thoughts with his acts. A mechanical scene follows in which the poets recite in turn, are whistled offstage by Caligula, and are then ordered to file out licking off any trace of their words from their writing tablets. After the humiliated poets, including his friend, Scipio, have left Caligula's presence, the emperor strangles Caesonia to death. Helicon is killed by an invisible hand. Finally, Caligula himself is murdered by the conspirators as he gazes into his mirror, uttering his last words: "To history, Caligula, to history . . . I am still alive!"— implying, apparently, that Caligula, or state terrorism, survives in man and is ever susceptible to renewed outbreaks.

The complex and ambiguous figure of Caligula—who, according to Camus, belongs to the rare species of "intelligent tyrants" endowed with a "certain grandeur"[1]—is a symbol of the despotic madness that denies existence to others and leads ultimately to one's own destruction. The number of corpses lying at the feet of the young emperor increases day by day (in this, he resembles the plague), until he is left utterly alone and then destroyed. His deliberate irrationality makes him a dadaistic figure, nihilistic in character and inevitably self-destroying.

The behavior of Caligula, the "imperial monster," has been interpreted as an indirect denunciation of totalitarianism and the German occupation, while his murderer, the tyrannicide Cherea, can be identified with the French resistance. Here again, however, one is dealing with a work begun long before World War II, and amid intellectual preoccupations of a quite different order. There are even indications that Camus at times regarded the bloodthirsty emperor as a kind of hero, because he dared to recognize and take up arms against the "absurdity" of the human condition. As is usual with Camus, however, the play contains various levels of meaning, which forbid one to see it as no more than a political allegory.

Completed toward the end of World War II, *Caligula* ranks as a tragedy in its violence of sentiments and cruelty of action, and the emperor may almost be regarded as a tragic hero in the sense that he perpetrates untold evil in the quest for an occult and unattainable good. The language of the play is lofty and pure, giving resonance to the complexity of its themes and holding in equilibrium the droll and the dark sides of its protagonist. Caligula sought his freedom by defying the heavens, but struck down other men in his attempt to achieve it. The question remains as to how man, either by challenging the gods who will his death or by himself becoming a god-man, can remain absolutely free without jeopardizing the sacredness of the life of others. Of all the works of Camus's "absurd" period, *Caligula* is the one that most successfully poses the problem to be pondered.

In a 1937 outline entry in his *Notebooks,* Camus had considered "Caligula or the Meaning of Death" as the preliminary title for the play. Almost symbolically, in 1960, a few days after the author's tragic death, the much-awaited staging of *Caligula,* directed by Sidney Lumet, premiered in a New York theater, where the empty seat in the first row had been reserved for Camus himself.

12

The Misunderstanding: Stark Realism

Like *Caligula, The Misunderstanding* was published in 1944 and once again reflects the somberness of the World War II era. The drama is based upon a story Camus had already recounted in *The Stranger*. Meursault, the central figure in that novel, discovers under the mattress in his prison cell a piece of yellowed newspaper containing an article about a man who left his native village in Czechoslovakia in order to seek his fortune in the world, and returned after twenty-five years as a rich man. Without disclosing his identity, the man went to lodge at the inn run by his mother and sister, to whom he has ostentatiously displayed his wealth. That night, he is beaten to death by the two women, who have stolen his money and thrown his body into the river. Too late, the man's wife has revealed the identity of their victim. The distraught mother hangs herself, while the crazed daughter commits suicide by throwing herself into a deep well. Meursault, who has read the article thousands of times during his imprisonment, expresses the view that while the tale was implausible it was also quite credible, and that in any case the traveler deserved his fate.

Camus made only minor changes in the story when he came to write *The Misunderstanding* in 1942–43. Far from his beloved Algeria, depressed by feelings of exile in a France encircled and occupied by the enemy, he incorporated into his play a sense of the hallucinating horrors Europe was then experiencing. In his preface, however, he asks that *The Misunderstanding* be interpreted not as an exercise in black fatalism but as a realistic play on the theme of revolt, the moral being that one must be straightforward and avoid ambiguity of speech. "If a man wants to be recognized, he simply has to say who he is."[1] If only the victim of the "misunderstanding" had adopted the sincerity and simplicity of language that Camus himself endeavored to practice throughout his life, he would have said to his mother, "Here I am, I am your son," and tragedy would have been averted.

As the play opens, the unsmiling Martha and her crime-weary mother are discussing the recently arrived guest, who is apparently wealthy, since he shows no concern about the price of the room he has engaged. From the dialogue between mother and daughter, the audience learns that he is destined to meet the same grisly fate as some of their earlier guests, thus bringing the two women closer to their goal of amassing enough money to escape "this land without horizon." Following their exit, Jan and his wife appear. Maria has not been presented to the mother and sister, and Jan is anxious that she leave quickly so they will continue to think he is alone; but Maria, having had a presentiment of evil, leaves him only reluctantly and shows no sympathy for the masquerade he has devised. In the ensuing conversation among the three family members, Jan learns that Martha and his mother no longer feel any affection for the "prodigal son," who is himself. Turning a deaf ear to Jan's words about "the heart," Martha is merely encouraged to proceed with the murderous plan that will enable her, she imagines, to leave her landlocked country and reach the sea.

In the second act, Martha, in making up the stranger's room, engages him in conversation about "Africa," his supposed place of origin, and waxes poetic about the misery of spring and autumn in Europe and the presumed delights of Africa's eternal summer. Then, turning hostile again, she leaves the stranger to the solitude and anxiety of his silent room. When she returns it is only to bring him a cup of heavily sedated tea. The guest falls into a deep sleep, and the two women, helped by the old deaf servant, proceed to steal his money and passport, then await the rising of the river that will enable them to drown the sleeping victim.

The accomplishment of their crime fills the loveless Martha with an elated eagerness to begin living at last; but her euphoria is abruptly dissipated at the beginning of act 3 when the old servant shows her the stolen passport that reveals Jan's true identity. Both women are shocked, and the mother, forcefully rejecting her daughter's appeal for a surrogate affection, cries out that "when a mother no longer recognizes a son, her role on earth is finished." Choosing to go to her punishment in hell, she commits suicide by drowning in the same river where the corpse of her son already lies. The fratricide Martha, now alone in her crime, will also commit suicide, but in the solitude of her room, without joining her dead brother and mother in the river, and without kneeling to reconcile herself with God.

In the final scene, Martha and Maria, the luckless wife, confront each other for the first and only time. In answer to Maria's expressions of grief and horror, Martha murmurs that there was a "misunderstanding." To deepen Maria's despair, she dilates upon the hideousness of human sympathy, the vanity of love, and the impossibility of recognizing one's brothers on an earth that is blanketed in darkness and where men are nothing but food for blind fish. In the violence of her outburst, Martha urges Maria to pray God that he will make her resemble a stone, for her choice in life now lies between the stupid happiness of a stone, and suicide. Maria, overwhelmed and fainting, with hands outstretched, calls out to God for pity. Ironically, it is the old deaf servant who takes notice: "Did you call me?" Maria turns toward him for help, but he refuses with a simple "No"—the word on which this totally negative play ends.

The characters in the play are five—a number that may be associated with the five fingers of the hand acting in unison or with the five fundamental laws of arithmetic, which imply a commutative and associative relationship among the characters. Though one of them, an old deaf servant, speaks only five devastating words at the end of the last act, the others converse quite copiously and in tragic, refined, and sometimes highly poetic language. The victim, Jan, is gentle and conciliatory. His sister, Martha, in contrast, is filled with the immense senselessness of hatred for others and solicitude for herself and her own happiness; while their mother, worn out and despairing, seeks some undefined and unattainable peace with almost religious tenacity. Jan's wife, Maria, is the diametric opposite of Martha. She loves Jan completely, is devastated by his absences, and desires nothing but to share his bed and clasp his hands. Both Martha, the cold-blooded murderess, and the virtuous and sensitive Maria, the very personification of love, can be identified with aspects of Camus himself. Both dream of a free life in a warm, sunny climate near the sea, and neither can be at ease amid the restrictions, the grayness, and the sadness of Europe—another example of the "sun and shadow" in Camus's personal makeup.

The very setting of The Misunderstanding—a cold, dreary inn where silence and hatred reign and men lie in ambush for each other—conveys a presentiment of bloodshed. It is a place where humans do not recognize other humans, where a "misunderstanding" can lead to fratricide and the killing of a son by his own mother. Realistically faithful to the details of life and to accurate representation without idealization, Camus has sharply delineated in this play a stark and sordid picture of an inhuman condition.

The Misunderstanding was first performed at the Théâtre des Mathurins in Paris on June 24, 1944, two months before the liberation of the French capital and at a time when the German military were still occupying orchestra seats. At the end of the performance, the actress playing the role of Martha (Maria Casarès, daughter of a minister of the Spanish Republic and Camus's favorite actress), stepped forward to announce that the play the troupe had just had the honor of presenting was by Albert Camus. Since Camus was known for his anti-Nazi sentiments, her announcement was intentionally provocative and probably occasioned the unfavorable terms in which the play was reviewed by a noted collaborationist critic.

Another accident of fortune was the banning of The Misunderstanding in Buenos Aires in 1949 because of its atheism, an action that provoked Camus to denounce the Peronist regime and to announce, during his South American trip, that he intended to boycott Argentina (see part VI, below).

13

State of Siege:
Land, Sea, Sky, and
Windscapes

State of Siege (1948) opens with the passing of a comet, believed by the citizens to be a portent of evil. Nada, the local idiot and drunkard, who scorns kings, comets, and morality, blaspheming and taking "liberties with God," declares that he, Nada, is above everything because he desires nothing. While the Choir celebrates pagan joys and the abundance of nature, Diego and Victoria, the young lovers, converse in highly poetic, declamatory language. Ending its declaration with a cry of joy, the Choir proceeds to adopt the status of "immobility" desired by the Governor. Utter stillness prevails until an actor, performing in a play within the play, collapses in full view of his public. The physician called to his aid announces "Plague!" Everyone moves about mechanically until the priest is heard summoning the crowd "To church!" where mimed confessions will be made at his urging. A man with a dazzling illuminated face predicts the end of the world in forty days, while a witch peddles her infallible potions among the people.

The scene shifts to the Palace, where the alcaides (governors or wardens), who are rejoicing that the plague has thus far been limited to the poor, heavily populated outskirts of the city, advise the Governor to withhold the truth from the citizens. The next scene takes place in the house of the Judge, who, concerned only about the safety of his son, orders his wife to stockpile enough food for the duration of the plague, after which they will lock themselves in their home without worrying about others—not even about their daughter, Victoria, who had not yet returned home. Victoria has been wandering through the streets of Cadiz in search of Diego, her lover, who, in a surgeon's mask, has already begun devoting himself to the sick and dying. In a grotesque encounter, Victoria exhorts Diego to remove his mask and kiss her passionately; he repels her and reveals his fear and horror of death, while the Choir chants, "Nothing is true but death."

Two strangers in uniform now appear: a Man and his female Secretary. To the Governor's query as to what they want, the Man replies: "Your place." In fact, he is the Plague personified, while his Secretary's function is to strike from her list of names those who must die. The governor, to save his own life and that of his alcaides, is obliged to hand over his powers to the strangers, announcing to the people that he has done so of his own free will. Messengers appear with new regulations for civil behavior. A black cross must be traced on the door of every infected household. Families who inform the authorities of the presence of a stricken person will be rewarded with a double food ration. All doors must be locked at 9:00 p.m. as the state of siege goes into effect. And since "words are a source of infection," every citizen must wear a vinegar-soaked gag over his mouth and keep silent.

The gagged population moves frantically toward the sea, seeking to escape the plague-ridden city before the gates are locked. Acts of vandalism flare; the priest flees, denying help to a beggar in need. Tensions mount as the gates close, one after another. When the last one finally closes, those remaining in Cadiz find themselves shut in "a black and red arena" in which the Plague now reigns supreme and is free to begin his round of ritual killings. A highly organized administration separates men from women; establishes that citizens will die and be incinerated afterwards—"or even before"; and gives notice that contaminated citizens will be marked with a bubonic star in their swollen inguinal regions and armpits.

Part 2 of *State of Siege* amounts to a caricatural satire on bureaucracy, "good citizenship," "elections," and incommunicability in the totalitarian state. Nada, the idiot, reappears, jumping gaily out of a heap of cadavers piled on a cart carrying the dead to the crematories. Nada's refrain is "Long live nothing—the only thing that exists." Since God denies the world, says Nada, he, Nada, denies God. The Choir laments the disappearance of Spain and of the winds that fail to rise to blow the plague away. Diego, now marked with the bubonic star, attempts to take refuge in the home of the Judge, who, however, tries to expel him because "it's the law." "But if the law is a crime?" Diego asks. The Judge retorts: "If crime becomes law, it ceases to be a crime"—thus summarizing the absurd politico-judiciary situation so characteristic of many modern dictatorships. Victoria presses herself to Diego, seeking to infect herself with the disease he bears within him, but he flees, bribing a boatman to take him to the ships anchored in the harbor outside the city walls. Just as he is about to jump into the boat that will take him to freedom, the Secretary appears to inform him that he is "listed." Approaching Diego seductively, she herself attempts to beguile him, but he revolts, refusing with all his might the infallible system of death she seeks to impose on the people of Cadiz. Diego actually slaps the Secretary, and the star suddenly disappears from his bubonic swellings, leading her to reveal that one man's revolt can slow down, although it cannot stop, the death machine. The efficacy of Diego's revolt symbolically takes the form of a rising of the winds, as the citizens remove their gags and lift their eyes to the skies.

In the third and last part of the play, Diego exhorts his fellow men to rise in revolt; but the Plague and the Secretary, confronted with growing popular disobedience, begin crossing out names at an accelerated rate. Some fall dead, but those who no longer fear do not die. In the ensuing battle between the Plague's soldiers and Diego's men, the list repeatedly changes hands. As each man takes possession of it, he crosses out the names of his own enemies, thus demonstrating the familiar principle that, given the opportunity, the oppressed become the oppressors in their turn. Catching sight of the dying Victoria lying on a stretcher, Diego offers his own life for hers. The Plague offers life to both of them if they will leave the city and allow him to reign supreme, but Diego refuses to abandon his men, who, together, finally succeed in freeing the city of the scourge. As the Plague withdraws in defeat, he nevertheless vaunts his superiority over "your God . . . who thought he could be powerful and good at the same time." Victoria rises from her stretcher, her life saved, but Diego, marked for death, falls and dies. The old order is now restored; as Nada will have it, "governments pass, the police remain." Declaring it impossible to live in the knowledge that "man is nothing and the face of God is horrible," Nada commits suicide by drowning in the sea.

Amid the deliberate diffuseness of this allegorical condemnation of arbitrary authority, the theme that stands out most prominently is that of revolt against death in the form of the plague. Its moral appears to be that only an act of revolt like that of the unfearing Diego can successfully combat this insidious, destructive force. Subsidiary themes have to do with the evils of unchecked political power, which insanely annihilates as many human beings as it deems necessary (represented by the Plague and the Secretary); the futility of nihilism and suicide (represented by the buffoon, Nada, symbol of absolute negation); and the high cost of freedom (represented by Victoria, who sacrifices herself to the man she loves and is saved only by his own sacrifice).

In his preface to this "spectacle in three parts," Camus warns that *State of Siege* (1948) is not a stage adaptation of his novel, *The Plague,* as one might suppose in view of its subject matter. This pageantlike production, developed in collaboration with actor and director Jean-Louis Barrault, has little in common with traditional dramatic structures. Ostensibly laid in the Spanish city of Cadiz, it mixes lyric monologue, simple dialogue, mime, farce, and choral recitation in a series of tableaux—the Palace, the Church, the Judge's home—which are accompanied by choral descriptions of the sea, the wind, and the parched land as seen from the city walls.

To the extent that it has any formal antecedents, *State of Siege* would seem to have been influenced by the *autosacramental* or allegorical drama of Spain's golden age in the sixteenth and seventeenth centuries. These popular representations gave dramatic form to abstract ideas in order to illustrate aspects of religious dogma through the use of allegory. Characters representing human types interacted with such abstractions as Pity, Charity, or the Devil. Essentially didactic in character, they established a precdent for the use of tendentious speeches, grandiloquence, alternating lyricism and propaganda, elements of farce, and an easily discernible morality.[1]

It is important to observe that, throughout the play, it is nature—

the seasons, the sea, and the skies—that gives people hope. To the cries of "Plague!" and "To church," the Choir counterpoises, "To the sea, to the sea!" symbolizing salvation. Only the sea can drown plagues, wars, and governments; only the sea offers "red mornings and green evenings perpetually." The sea is the "water of hope," and its cool breeze lifts men's hearts. When the city is in the grip of the plague, the winds die down and the sky is empty; when the plague is driven out by fresh winds, rain falls on the dry land and winter is succeeded, miraculously, by an abundant "autumn when all grows green again."

As in so many of his works, Camus relieves the starkness of death and destruction through a lyrical invocation of his love of nature and his deep conviction that the sun, the sea, the sky, and the wind are part of man's salvation.

14

The Just Assassins:
Expressionism

The Just Assassins (1950), a drama of the Russian revolutionary movement, was fairly successful in its original production and in subsequent revivals, but has been criticized on the score of excessive wordiness, lack of onstage action, and weakness in its portrayal of the lovers. If, however, one takes to heart the heroine's words to her companion—that they are not lovers in this world, because the warmth of love is not for the "just"—it becomes apparent that the play is primarily concerned with Camus's political thought and, from that point of view, it may be considered one of his most mature and compelling works.

Unfolding in five well-structured acts, the drama opens on a scene in the year 1905, in which three apparently young and well-educated Russian terrorists, Dora, Annenkov, and Stepan, are plotting the assassination of the Grand Duke Sergei, uncle of the czar. The three form a combat group of the revolutionary socialist party, which is dedicated to the liberation of all Russians and to the practice of terrorism until the land is returned to the people. Their comrade, Voinov, enters, with plans of the route the grand duke's carriage will follow from the palace to the theater. Voinov's presence in the revolutionary ranks dates from his expulsion from the university because of his statement that Peter the Great had built Saint Petersburg "with blood and whip." From that experience, Voinov had concluded that it was not enough simply to denounce injustice, but that one must combat it even at the cost of one's own life.

Though each of the terrorists would like to be selected for the honor of assassinating the grand duke, their leader, Annenkov, chooses one of their number, Kaliayev, to throw the bomb. He also orders that in case the bomb fails, Kaliayev is not to take the alternative course of throwing himself under the horses in an attempt to assure the grand duke's death. Annenkov wants no suicides; even if he fails, Kaliayev must continue in his terrorism. The idealistic Kaliayev, who feels that to die for an idea is the only way to rise to its height and justify it, nevertheless hopes to find his death in the assassination attempt. Dora, too, would like to die in one of the bombing attacks, but she also cherishes a vision of even greater felicity in the form of a condemnation to die upon the scaffold. This, for her, would give a twofold meaning to life, first in the terroristic act itself, and the again on the scaffold, with "the eternal wait between the two." Dora expresses her fear that Kaliayev will falter when he finds himself actually face-to-face with his victim; but Kaliayev is confident that his hatred will blind him to the sobering fact that he is actually killing a man.

The second act, however, vindicates Dora's doubts. Kaliayev's hand has been paralyzed by an unforeseen circumstance, the presence in the carriage of the grand duke's children as well as the intended victim. Weeping over his failure, Kaliayev promises to return to the theater to carry out his assignment at the end of the performance. The militant Stepan, who earlier had expressed mistrust of Kaliayev and suspicion of his "love for life," sarcastically mocks "the poet" for having failed in his duty to obey orders, and accuses him of lukewarm belief in the aims of the revolution. He himself, Stepan confesses, hates his fellow men and is committed to the revolution because he loves not life but "the justice which stands above life." Kaliayev, repelled by the despotic quality in Stepan's thought, retorts that men do not live by justice alone, but by justice coupled with innocence. To kill children, he declares, is contrary to honor; and if the revolution shies from honor, he, Kaliayev, will no longer remain a revolutionary. Although willing to return to the theater to throw the bomb that will kill the children as well as the grand duke, he will then unhesitantly carry out the suicidal gesture of throwing himself under the horses. Annenkov, however, has by this time decided that the murder of the children is unnecessary, and postpones the assassination attempt for two days—a riskier solution, but one that will limit the killing to the grand duke alone. Kaliayev has won his point.

In the third act, Dora and Kaliayev declare their love for one another—a tormented love, linked to the organization, prisons, and justice, the impossible love of "just" men and women. Act 4 finds Kaliayev already in prison, having meanwhile succeeded in the second assassination attempt and spent eight days in solitary confinement. Proudly, he declares himself be a prisoner of war and refuses a proffered pardon, maintaining that the bomb he threw was directed against tyranny, not against a man. The police chief, using an argument that might have been borrowed from *The Rebel*—namely, that one begins by wanting justice and ends up by organizing a police force—offers Kaliayev his life and that of his comrades if he will only repent and denounce his associates. Kaliayev, however, is adamant in his refusal; nor is his resolve shaken by a visit and personal appeal from the widowed grand duchess. The police chief, hoping to deceive Kaliayev's comrades into a belief that he has betrayed them, publishes a report of his interview with the grand duchess in which it is stated that the terrorist has in fact repented.

The last act of the play focuses on the skepticism of the organization's members regarding Kaliayev's supposed repentance, and on Dora's despairing doubts about the rightness of their path, strewn as it is with the corpses of their victims. For Dora, as for Camus himself, the right path leads toward life and sun, whereas their route has led to death and constant cold. Though she remains faithful to the revolutionary cause, Dora's heart, which was light when she joined the group, is now sad and imprisoned. Realizing that it is easier to die than to live amid such contradictions, she seeks and obtains from her comrades the privilege of throwing the next bomb. In serving the revolutionary cause, as she believes, her act will also lead to her reunion in death with the condemned Kaliayev.

The controlled tone and realistic dialogue of *The Just Assassins,* with its powerful portrayal of the type of the "rebel" who kills in a just cause and is willing to sacrifice his own life in return, makes the play an effective stage vehicle and a compelling objectification of some of Camus's deepest thoughts on justice and the taking of human life. In one of his *Notebooks* jottings, Camus had written that, for Kaliayev, "murder coincides with suicide. . . . One life is paid for by another"—adding, however, that the value of a life that is snatched from its owner is less than that of a life offered in sacrifice.

Though based on historical events and characters, *The Just Assassins* cannot be considered a historical play, for it is clearly Camus's intention to counterpoise the reasons of the heart against the pitiless requirements of a revolution ostensibly aimed at relieving human misery. From this point of view, it is a form of expressionism that is concerned less with objective reality than with the subjective emotions and responses that events rouse in an artist.

It is impossible to be sure how far, if at all, Camus associates himself with the thinking of his more militant revolutionary characters, whose political naïveté and cocksure morality are only a shade less repellent than the grim self-righteousnes of the murderous Martha in *The Misunderstanding*. The fact that these revolutionaries believe their cause to be "just" cannot excuse their myopic self-deception or their ruthless disregard for the very values they profess to champion.

At the same time, Camus cannot blind himself to the real evils against which their activities are directed, however misguidedly. Herein lies the tragic dilemma: does one side with the upholders of an evil status quo or with those who would violently attack it? Camus's own feelings, in face of this dilemma, are perhaps best reflected in the phrase, "Neither victims nor executioners," the title of a series of articles he contributed to the newspaper *Combat* in 1948.

The tragic conflict in this play thus lies not in the occasional discords among the more militant terrorists, but in the inner struggle, the doubts, and torments in the hearts of the hero and the heroine.[1] Kaliayev and Dora are "delicate murderers," whose troubled consciences vacillate between respect for life and love on the one hand, and what to them seems the cruel necessity of killing. In their dilemma, *The Just Assassins* offers a succinct summary of Camus's political and humanistic thought. The terrorist undertakes to carry out the crime of murder in anticipation of a splendid future for humanity—a world in which killing would no longer exist. His accomplice lucidly returns his argument: "And supposing it doesn't turn out that way?"

Among all the literary and artistic media in which Albert Camus employed his talents, it was the theater that he found most congenial to his abilities and temperament. This was true not only because of its quality of vividness and immediacy, of direct, reciprocal communication between actors and audience, but also because of the feeling of teamwork and solidarity uniting the people involved in any theatrical production. Camus's translations and adaptations of works for the stage, no less than his own dramatic output, bear witness to this continuing enthusiasm.

Of Camus's four dramatic works, two were completed and performed during World War II and two others date from the early postwar years. All of them are concerned in one way or another with death or killing, and are all imbued with the somberness that also characterizes the novels and essays of the period, from *The Stranger* and *The Myth of Sisyphus* to *The Plague* and *The Rebel.* They offer no more than an occasional distant glimpse of the joy in living, the unity with nature so prevalent in the works of Camus's earlier years and occasionally recaptured in his final decade.

Caligula and *The Misunderstanding,* the two plays presented near the end of World War II, are closely related in theme and spirit to the other works of Camus's "absurdist" period. Both dramas seem intent on demonstrating the vacuity and meaninglessness of human existence, *Caligula* through the crimes and vagaries of a mad Roman emperor, *The Misunderstanding* through the futility of a cold-blooded murder by two women whose victim turns out to be their own son and brother. In *State of Siege* Camus had progressed from the pure absurd to the concept of revolt, and has shown how the forces of evil—symbolized, as in *The Plague,* by a mysterious pestilence—may be checked, if not quelled, by a spontaneous act of resistance. Finally, in *The Just Assassins* (1950), Camus's study of the terrorist underground in prerevolutionary Russia explores the ethical and human questions involved in the use of political murder as a weapon against tyranny.

The reader will at some point become aware of an unresolved

problem in regard to Camus's attitude toward the taking of human life—a problem that occurs not only in the plays but also in such novels as *The Stranger* and the still earlier *A Happy Death*. That unfinished story begins with a murder deliberately carried out by the main character for the sole purpose of obtaining funds to support a more satisfactory life-style. It is impossible to believe that Camus, essentially humane and passionately opposed to capital punishment, could approve of such actions. Yet he treats them with such seeming casualness that an incautious reader might well impute to him an attitude not unlike that of his own Caligula, who seems to regard the killing of other human beings as a legitimate and proper form of self-expression.

The problem becomes especially difficult in *The Just Assassins*, where, as the title suggests, the assassins are motivated by a rather naïve but passionately held ideal of justice. Is Camus saying that killing is legitimate if only one convinces oneself that it is being done in a good cause? Such reasoning would legitimize any number of political assassinations in this and earlier centuries. Or is he pointing up an underlying tension between ends and means—in this case, between the desire for an ultimate good and the temptation to pursue it by the wrong methods? This is one of the fundamental questions to which Camus himself supplies no explicit answer. His very reticence enhances the endless fascination of his work and personality.

As in the novels and essays, Camus again ponders in the plays the role in society of judges and juries, as well as the validity of human or divine judgments. The bloodthirsty Caligula constitutes himself as the sole supreme official authorized to decide questions of life and death, and he sits in judgment on gods and men. Mother and daughter, the self-appointed executioners in *The Misunderstanding*, are blind to extenuating circumstances and deny their victim—their own son and brother—even a glimmer of hope. In *State of Seige*, Camus is articulate in denouncing the Judge as the total negation of a rigorously professional conception of the judicial office, for this Judge favors his son to the detriment of his daughter, refuses asylum to the refugee from terrorism, Diego, and hoards, for his own survival, supplies of food lifted from the citizens of Cadiz. Kaliayev, the just assassin, kills the grand duke and the hangman of the czarist state kills Kaliayev; is one, or neither, or are both guilty of injustice and of taking human life? The dilemma remains. Each man "bears about / A silent court of justice in his breast, / Himself the judge and jury, and himself / The prisoner at the bar, ever condemn'd" (Alfred Tennyson, *Sea Dreams*).

Part V

The Short Stories

I do not think that any of the six tales contained in *Exile and the Kingdom* can be ranked with Albert Camus's most accomplished writings; but no other book by Camus has made me more keenly aware of the profound nature and actual status of his work. The quest, the intensity, the distribution of this work; what it has attempted and still is attempting to do; what new horizons open up before it: all seem to me to be more clearly visible here than anywhere else.

—Gaëtan Picon, "Exile and the Kingdom"

15

Exile and the Kingdom: A Diorama

The six short stories that compose *Exile and the Kingdom* (1957) vary in composition and structure from the realistic tale to the interior monologue. A seventh story, *The Fall*, it may be remembered, was originally intended for inclusion in this collection, but eventually became a novel in itself.

Like the image of the dead rat in the opening of *The Plague*, the desperate buzzing of a trapped fly in the first sentence of "The Adulterous Woman" conveys a premonitory sense of exasperation and unpleasantness. The woman of the title is Janine, a heavy, fleshy, still-desirable housewife whose husband, Marcel, a resident of Algiers, is interested only in his cloth business. Despite his banal personality, Janine admires his courage in facing the uncertainties of life in North Africa where the effects of the war have severely cut into his trade. Having decided that he must now dispense with middlemen and sell directly to the Arab merchants in the villages of the southern plateau, Marcel is traveling southward with his wife on a bus crowded with Arabs, through the penetrating cold of the Algerian desert—a far cry from the warmth and beauty of the palm trees that Janine had naïvely expected. Their destination is an insignificant Arab town where they will lodge in a small, cold hotel room that reminds the reader of Jan's cold, impersonal room in *The Misunderstanding*. In this story, too, there will be a failure of understanding between husband and wife, though not of the same tragic proportions as in the drama.

Before retiring, Marcel and Janine visit the ramparts of the town's fortress, from which they are able to contemplate the desert's endless

expanse. From her vantage point, Janine sees sky and earth joined in a "pure line," where something unexpected seems to await her. She reflects on the existence of the desert nomads—servants of no men, poor, but free lords in this strange kingdom. For a fleeting instant, their kingdom is hers, and she experiences a burst of exaltation.

That night, in their hotel room, Janine grasps her sleeping husband's shoulder. He is unresponsive, as always. Realizing that there is no love between them, and impelled by a strange, interior force, she slips out and hurries through the sleeping town to the parapet of the fortress where she can contemplate the bright stars that reunite her with her deepest self. After so many years of fleeing both herself and her fears—perhaps symbolized by the fly that sought to escape through the closed windows of the bus—she now stops to find her roots. Lying on the ground, Janine gives herself up to nature. "The water of the night" fills her recumbent body. Her return to the hotel and to the marital bed awakens her husband, who turns on a light that "slaps her full in the face." Try as he will, Marcel is unable to fathom why Janine is weeping so uncontrollably.

The second story, "The Renegade," is almost unbearably painful to read because of the implacable cruelty of the actions described. It is the interior monologue of an anguished and confused mind, in a mutilated and tortured body and in a setting of almost unbelievable harshness and barbarity. A "dirty slave," a onetime priest whose tongue has been cut out of his mouth and whose body is covered with open, salted wounds, waits in ambush under the burning sun of the Sahara Desert for a missionary priest whom he is determined to kill.

A brute in his youth in France, this man had been led to believe that Catholicism was the path to the sun and clear waters. Now, however, he feels that he was totally deceived, and he intends to settle accounts by killing the European missionary who is being sent out to replace him. The Catholic seminary had ostensibly prepared him to preach the gospel to the barbarian inhabitants of a town closed to strangers and peopled by savages. But on reaching the "cold, torrid city," whose denizens ruled ferociously over the black slaves who worked the salt mines, he had been taken by the guards, beaten, exposed in the town's square, then conveyed to the "house of the fetish," the temple-prison where he was horribly tortured and forced to take part in grotesque ceremonies in adoration of the resident god. This barbaric deity he now hails as his only god and master, adoring it as the earth's wicked principle. The concept of love had served simply to betray him, he feels; only the kingdom of evil has no flaws or cracks in it. The day his tongue was cut out, he learned to adore "the immortal soul of hatred."

Once the killing of the new missionary has been accomplished, however, the concept of absolute evil appears to the renegade as no less futile than that of the absolute good that was taught him at the seminary. A voice within clamors for a new kingdom of hope, but his own death is now approaching rapidly, and he is left, his mouth crammed with salt, desperately suspended between extinction and uncertainty. The message that Camus delivers in this traumatizing manner appears to be concerned with the dubiety of absolutes and the need to limit one's search for a truth, or an object of reverence, to the human realm within reach. Catholicism and fetishism are alike repudiated; neither the one nor the other, for Camus, represents the position of tolerance and moderation that he seeks. The nonexistent kingdom of the "cold, torrid city," itself a contradiction in terms, also stands in contradiction to the basic reverence for life that Camus proffered as the sole possibility for relative happiness.

"The Silent Man" tells a simpler story, again with a North African setting. Yvars, a cooper, who bicycles to his work each morning, his back to the sea, is growing old and looking forward to nothing more than gazing at the sea as he pedals his way home each evening to a glass of anisette on the terrace of his house. Yvars does not know whether he is happy or sad; he only knows that he must wait, without knowing for what. The workers in the small barrel factory where he works, and which Camus describes in the minutest detail, have gone on strike but lost. The owner, who has had to reduce his costs because of the inroads of advanced technology, is not hard-hearted but rather paternalistic in his outlook, even though he did respond to the strikers' initiative with a lockout. The resentful workers finally return to their jobs, but refuse to speak to the owner until the moment when his small daughter is taken by ambulance to the hospital and they feel impelled to express their human concern. It is of the little girl that Yvars thinks as he cycles home that evening. In the final scene, a compassionate Yvars, holding his wife's hand,

watches the swift twilight running over the sea's horizon and wishes
for the youth and strength that would permit him to follow it. Once
again, Camus uses the image of the sea to symbolize escape to
freedom and to happiness.

The fourth story, "The Guest," focuses on Daru, the teacher in a
isolated schoolhouse on the edge of the Algerian desert. He watches
two approaching figures, one on horseback, one on foot. Balducci,
the gendarme, is the mounted man. His companion, hands bound
behind his back, is an Arab prisoner who has unintentionally killed
his cousin in a dispute over some grain. Daru prepares tea for the
pair, then learns that he himself is expected to take charge of the
prisoner and hand him over the following morning to the authorities
of the nearby town of Tinguit. The gendarme gives Daru a revolver
to protect himself; but the latter determines, after some reflection,
that he will not obey the order. To do so, he feels, would be
"dishonorable," for in this desert solitude, there is a bond of fraternity between men. This sense of human solidarity, for Daru at least,
continues to evolve as the two men pass the night in the darkened
room. A moment of suspense is created by the Arab's silent rising
from his bed; he does not, however, try either to escape or to take
possession of the revolver.

The next morning, Daru prepares coffee, food, and money for his
"guest"; then, accompanying him to the crossroads, he shows him
the way to Tinguit, where the authorities await him, but leaves him
free to escape if he cares to do so. The taciturn Arab, nevertheless,
chooses the road to Tinguit of his own accord. Returning to the
schoolhouse, Daru finds scrawled on the blackboard the words:
"You handed over our brother. You will pay." The story closes on
the image of a crushed Daru, oppressed by solitude and isolation.
"In this country which he loved so much, he was alone"—a sentence
that encapsulates, as only Camus could do, the tragic misunderstanding among the protagonists in the Algerian conflict.

The fifth story, "The Artist at Work," tells a satirically realistic
tale of a famous Parisian artist, Jonah, and of the lucky star that
never failed him until, to use a biblical analogy, he is cast from the
ship of society and swallowed up in a place of exile. Jonah himself
knows little about art, but has many disciples who "teach their
master," explaining to him what he paints and why. His reputation

gains in proportion as his actual work decreases, until the sad day when his lucky star sets. He sells fewer and fewer paintings; his patron reduces his royalties; and, to the distress of his wife, he takes to wine and women. Finally, having decided to build himself a flimsy studio under the high ceiling of their overcrowded apartment (the belly of Jonah's great fish?), he works in darkness, meditates, takes his meals alone, and sleeps away from his wife and children. The closing scene finds Jonah working feverishly, day and night, on a mysterious canvas, until he finally collapses. The physician assures his family that he will survive, however, and his friends find on the blank canvas one single, incomplete word: is it *solitary* or *solidarity?*

This tale shows keen awareness of the plight of the successful artist (or writer) in contemporary society. In order to create, he must strike a balance between his need for solitude and for solidarity with others; yet he may all too readily find himself unable to produce because of family problems, inadequate working space, and the importunities and selfishness of friends, visitors, and disciples. Talent, success, and glory besiege the unhappy artist, whose life seems governed by the terrible paradox that calm can only be restored if he, like his biblical namesake, is thrown overboard and swallowed by a great fish.

"The Growing Stone"—the last tale in *Exile and the Kingdom*—is set in the tropics of Brazil and concerns the visit of a French engineer, D'Arrast, to the poverty-stricken riverside town of Iguape to supervise the building of a dam that will end the periodic flooding of the settlement. He visits the wretched hut of one of the indigent, half-pagan families, and the grotto where an effigy of the Good Jesus had been brought and washed by the fishermen who found it. The grotto also contains a talisman or fetish that is considered highly efficacious against infirmities, shipwreck, and other calamities—a "growing stone," one that continues to grow even though slivers are constantly being cut off by pious pilgrims. A mulatto ship's cook, who has been saved at sea by the light from the dome of the Church of the Good Jesus, has vowed to carry a block of stone weighing fifty kilograms on his head, in thanks for his rescue, in a religious procession set for the following day.

A bond of fraternity soon develops between D'Arrast and this cook, who escorts him that night to a native ceremony similar to one observed by Camus during his visit to South America in 1949. The crowded hut contains an altar decorated with a chromolithograph of Saint George and the dragon, as well as a red statue of a horned pagan god carrying a silver paper knife. Ritual dances are performed, and some of the participants experience trances and convulsions. D'Arrast is almost overcome by the heat and smoke and his own exertions in executing an immobile dance with the weight of his own body. Eventually he is asked to leave, but the cook stays on, forgetful of the vow he is to execute the following morning.

Tired out after a night of dancing, the cook walks haltingly in the next day's procession, his body trembling under the great block of stone on his head. He finally falls to the ground, exhausted and weeping over his failure to fulfill his vow. To the amazement of the crowd, the husky D'Arrast steps forward and lifts the stone onto his own shoulders. Instead of heading for the church, however, he defiantly struggles to reach the wretched hut he had visited earlier. Here he drops the stone in the middle of the floor, exhausted in his turn but flooded with an obscure and undefinable joy. It seems to D'Arrast, as he joins the family circle of the poor inhabitants, that his life is beginning anew, with a new force that gives him an identity in the larger universe. His success in performing an almost superhuman task on behalf of a fellow man gives a heretofore unknown meaningfulness to D'Arrast's existence, as well as offering a moving tribute to the poverty-stricken town of Iguape.

The loneliness of the individual, the sense of foreignness in one's own land and of isolation in one's own society, is the underlying theme of the six short stories that make up *Exile and the Kingdom*, Camus's sole venture in this literary genre. Despite their narrative form, these carefully wrought vignettes are closely akin to some of Camus's essays in their brilliant evocation of particular scenes, special moments of time, and states of mind that rivet the reader's attention in spite of the comparative slightness of the action.

In these mature works, Camus appears for the most part to have left behind the darkness and violence of the war and postwar years, and to acknowledge at least a possibility of transcending the crippling limitations of everyday life. Counterpoised to the theme of

"Exile" is that of "the Kingdom," equated by Camus with a certain "free and naked way of life" that must be recaptured if one is to be reborn. Exile, he seems to be saying, points the way to reintegration into this "kingdom of man," a status that several of his characters appear to attain in at least a momentary and provisional sense. Along this pathway to redemption, Camus warns with a certain characteristic sternness, one must reject both slavery on the one hand and "possession" on the other.

In contrast to the power-crazed characters in Camus's theater, the various personages of *Exile and the Kingdom* illustrate primarily the muted struggle of oppressed figures in everyday life, rather than some mythical existence. They are victims rather than executioners—victims to whom no clearly defined form of revolt is offered.[1] Living out their varied states of confusion, bewilderment, weakness, muddled reality, and divided loyalties, they have in common a certain kindness of heart—except, perhaps, for the "renegade," in whom all human feeling is extinct—which refuses to exclude other men from a fraternal company. Camus had acknowledged, in *The Wrong Side and the Right Side,* that he was linked to the rest of the world by all of his acts, to all men by his pity and gratitude. *Exile and the Kingdom* gives the best possible expression to his inner feeling of malice toward none and charity for all.

In a diorama of translucent North African, European, and South American scenes, the figures of Janine, of the renegade, of Yvars, Daru, Jonah, and D'Arrast stand out lifelike against their realistic backgrounds, which range from the arid splendor of the silent desert to the rushing river of a tropical forest. The viewer cannot fail to savor the artistically dramatic effects of the display as well as the bits of human experience for which it serves as backdrop.

Part VI

Notebooks and *American Journals*

Camus opted neither for stoicism nor ascetism, but rather for the realization and acceptance of the notion of *"nothingness as the essence of life."* Such an approach to existence enabled him to experience and understand the discord and the harmony inherent within the human personality and the world at large. To look upon the mysteries of life in the world and in the galaxies . . . did not fill him with a sense of utter despair. What is remarkable in terms of Camus's writings is that hopelessness became a positive factor in his world, inviting him to get used to his own loneliness, thereby strengthening him, encouraging him to proceed courageously through the harrowing events making up the life experience. Camus remarked . . . that the very moment a person is struck down by despair, amazingly enough, *"thirst is reborn,"* filling the individual with a livingness—a need for growth and fulfillment.

—Bettina L. Knapp, in her introduction to
Critical Essays on Albert Camus

16

Notebooks and *American Journals*:[1]
Gray on Gray

Camus the man, as well as the artist, emerges clearly and attractively from the often disjointed, sometimes cryptic *Notebook* entries. Determined atheist though he is and will remain, he reveals a fraternal feeling for that fellow lover of the sun, Saint Francis of Assisi, devotee of poverty, nature, and life. Camus, too, dwells at length on his need for asceticism and beauty as well as his own deep sense of a duty to love. Uncovering unsuspected aspects of himself in a highly revelatory and moving style, he also describes his illness and his reactions to its progress, as well as his personal feelings during his periods of convalescence in France. Also documented in the jottings are Camus's exhausting battles against the double temptation of cynicism and suicide. In the later brief notes, repeated allusions to nihilism and despair, imagistic splashes of blood, evocations of cemeteries, and an awareness of approaching death gradually close in on a tired, ill, depressed, and anguished man.

Camus's expressions of nostalgic longing for the Algerian sun and the sensuous Mediterranean light produce some of his most unforgettable paragraphs. Through the *Notebooks* flash images of the sun, the sea, the hills of Europe, Africa, North and South America, which are contrasted with the melancholy grayness of Paris and New York as Camus saw them. Numerous are the phrases in which the sea is equated with sensuality, life, and eternity. Deep are the antinomies struck between sun and darkness, between the sensuousness of Mediterranean nature and the dead steel and concrete

135

of northern cities. What absurdity, Camus explains, to leave the sea and the sun and go north to find stone, rain, solitude, and anguish! He laments man's reckless effacement of nature, calling it the "modern cancer," and notes with sad irony that landscapes are gradually disappearing from his own *Notebooks* as the entries accumulate.

The *Notebooks* contain many impressions of places Camus had visited, indications of trips in the offing, and his feelings about travel. He clearly does not enjoy traveling, and the very notion of "pleasure travel" is alien to him. Especially in northern countries, he felt a chronic uneasiness, due partly to his intensely Mediterranean consciousness and his habit of carrying with him, on all his travels, the memories and predilections of his original milieu.

More connected jottings on his trips to North and South America were extracted from the *Notebooks* and published separately, in France as *Journaux de voyage* in 1978 and in the United States as *American Journals* in 1987. Having gained sufficient celebrity to be in demand as a lecturer and literary lion in the countries of the New World, Camus set out for New York on March 10, 1946, traveling ostensibly as a journalist. Preferring to spend most of his time on deck rather than in his overcrowded cabin, he was fascinated by the mixture of water and moonlight in the ship's wake—"liquid marble" in one image, and, in the next, a fine lace that is repeatedly worked and then unraveled. Throughout the *American Journals,* Camus keeps seeking an appropriate metaphor for the "blooming" of water and light, a "continuous symbol," combining and recombining in constantly changing configurations.

The first glimpse of New York—"hideous human city"—fills his heart with trembling at the thought of such admirable "inhumanity," with its implications of power, order, and economic strength. Though prepared to change his initial opinion later on, he finds no reason to do so. After a visit to Washington, D.C., where he saw long-legged girls whose splendid faces were devoid of love, his diary entry is curt: "I have suddenly ceased to be curious about this country."

In New York, he is continually struck by details: gloved garbage collectors, orderly traffic, long blocks of bridal shops in the Bowery, juxtaposed with scenes of the utmost misery, and the impression that everyone looks as though he had stepped out of a film. Broadway is a "luminous fair" whose violent lights stultify him; he realizes he had reached a "new continent," because *real* smoke comes out of the mouth of a soldier smoking a Camel cigarette in a fifteen-meter-high billboard in Times Square. He admires the magnificent food shops, the women and their bright dresses, and the color of the taxis, which look like insects dressed up for Sunday in reds, greens, and yellows; but he is horrified by necktie shops with a concentration of bad taste that is scarcely imaginable. He is puzzled by the function of the Funeral Home and the fact that cemeteries are private property where space is reserved in advance. Thousands of operetta generals and admirals catch his eye: they are New York's doormen, bell captains, and elevator boys in the big hotels.

One of Camus's best-contrived images is his personification of New York's elevated railway train, speeding along out of the Bowery, surrounded by slowly dancing skyscrapers. The machine swallows up little red and blue lights, allows itself to be digested momentarily by the stations, and then speeds off again into the poorer neighborhoods beyond Manhattan. One can easily imagine Camus, a lonely nocturnal passenger, desperately peering out of the train window and vainly searching for the panchromatic nature of his beloved Algeria.

East Orange and the surrounding New Jersey countryside are a "pretty postcard," with thousands of clean cottages, nestled like toys among poplars and magnolia trees. Traveling from New York to Canada, he catches sight of little and big homes with white columns and lawns unseparated by any kind of fence, so that the impression is of one big lawn that belongs to everyone, and where children laugh and play. As for Maine and New England, his only diary entry is "land of lakes and red houses"; while Canada is a big, calm, slow country, oblivious to the recent war, and Montreal, with its two hills, on a Sunday afternoon, fills him with "Ennui. Ennui." Quebec, on the other hand, offers a thrilling impression of beauty and grandeur. The "prodigious landscape" of Cape Diamond and the Saint Lawrence River are characterized as air, light, and water merging in infinite proportions.

Although Camus found Americans to be generous, hospitable,

and cordial, he was oppressed from the moment of his arrival by an indefinable *"tragique américain,"* which, at the same time, seemed unconscious of itself. "Afternoon with some students. They don't feel the real problem, and yet their unhappiness is obvious. In this country where *everything* is directed to proving that life is not tragic, they have the sense of something lacking. This great effort is pathetic, but one must reject the tragic *after* having contemplated it, not before."

The same sense of something lacking was to obsess Camus during his visit to South America to deliver a series of lectures in the summer of 1949. For him the trip was a depressing experience, physically and psychologically, from the moment he boarded the vessel at Marseilles after an exhausting drive in his automobile, "Desdemona." This time he was at least assigned a single cabin, but the South Atlantic crossing was marred by fever, loneliness, and social constraints. The other passengers were a strange assortment, whose conversation was of very little interest. Admitting that his impulses were directed not toward human beings but toward the sea, his diary entries often sum up his social encounters in one word— "sad." Sometimes he took refuge in the crowded fourth-class lounge, to watch the immigrants' drinking and singing; among them, he felt happy "for ten seconds." His preference was to watch the ocean from the ship's deck, rising early in the morning to work in the sun on the lectures he was to deliver in South America.

A character wholly antithetical to Camus and his love for color, nakedness, and the sea, was the passenger who, even under the tropical sun, was dressed in a dark gray suit, stiff-collared shirt, and black shoes. Trailing him four times around the deck, Camus noted that he never once looked at the sea. What more scathing judgment could be pronounced?

The ship crossed the Tropic of Cancer, "under a vertical sun that kills all shadows," and Camus was happy on the following day, during a stopover in Dakar, to find again the "smell of my Africa, smell of misery and abandon, virgin smell, and strong, whose seductiveness I know." The equator was crossed on July 10, but the usual ceremonies were omitted because most of the passengers had disembarked at Dakar. The twenty-odd who remained were treated instead to a Laurel and Hardy film. Camus took refuge in the ship's bow to contemplate the moon and the Southern Cross. How few and anemic were the stars in these southern skies, he observed, compared to Algeria's nights, "swarming with stars."

With no land visible, the long days between Dakar and Rio were spent in prolonged contemplation of the ocean and in work on his lectures. The lights of Rio de Janeiro and Sugarloaf Mountain finally came into view on July 15, together with the immense and "regrettable" luminous Christ on the highest mountain top, Corcovado. In Rio, Camus was again pleased to find himself completely alone in a charming room of the French ambassadorial residence. His first notations, on the day of arrival, concern Brazilian motorists, who are "happy madmen or cold sadists." He was impressed by the harsh contrast between the luxury of the fine hotels and modern buildings and the poverty of the *favelas,* where a miserable black and white population lived without water or electricity. All in all, the mountains, the bay, the sultry air, and the stars over Rio made him more melancholy than happy.

As time went on, Camus became increasingly exasperated by formalities, the shortcomings of the diplomatic services responsible for his travel arrangements, the delegations that failed to meet his planes. The climate was oppressive, and he was frequently ill. He relates his peregrinations sometimes with tongue in cheek, but more often with ill humor and biting sarcasm.

Perhaps the only city he really enjoyed was Recife, at Brazil's eastern tip, "the Florence of the tropics," as he called it. The nearby historic town of Olinda, with its old churches and beautiful Franciscan monastery, also appealed to him, but he returned to his hotel shaking with fever.

One redeeming feature of the stay in Brazil was the opportunity to observe some of the exotic rites that blended Roman Catholicism with traditional African practices, as he was later to describe them in "The Growing Stone." At Caxias, a village forty kilometers from Rio, he witnessed a *macumba,* a night-long ceremony whose participants, having become possessed by a god, sought to enter a trancelike condition through dances and songs conducted under the guidance of a priest and principal dancer, who was known as the "father of the saints." Wedged into an overcrowded mud-and-straw hut, Camus watched the ceremony unfold to its climax, but left at two in the morning after being told it would continue until dawn. Coming out into the cool night air, he observed succinctly that he preferred the night and the sky to the gods of men.

A *bomba-menboi*, which Camus found "quite extraordinary," was witnessed in Recife. It, too, was of religious origin, but its dances were diabolical in character. Camus described it as a kind of grotesque ballet, executed by masked and totemic figures, its unvarying theme the killing of a bull that is then reborn to carry off a young girl between its horns.

In the fishing village of Itapoa (Bahia), with its straw huts, beautiful untouched beaches, and foaming sea bordered by coconut groves, Camus was able to view a third such ceremony, this one a *candomblé* danced by richly costumed women led by a matron, in contrast to the all-male character of the *macumba*. Executed in front of a table laden with food, the dancelike ceremony was accompanied by three drums and a flattened funnel struck by an iron bar. A group of young black girls entered the scene in a semihypnotized state; watching their rythmic dance, Camus became enraptured by the infinite grace of one of them whom he dubbed a "black Diana."

Most remarkable of all was the pilgrims' procession to the "growing stone" at Iguape, three hundred kilometers and ten hours from São Paulo over roads covered with red dust and dry mud. The essential features of the visit are related in *Exile and the Kingdom* (see Part V, above).

After visits to Fortaleza and Porto Alegre, Camus left Brazil for Montevideo, Uruguay, a city he found attractive with its necklace of boardwalks and beaches and whose mimosas and palm trees reminded him of Menton on the French Rivera. He boarded a steamer the following evening for the overnight journey across the Rio de la Plata to Buenos Aires, the capital of Argentina—a metropolis "of rare ugliness" that he had originally intended to bypass in response to the banning of his play, *The Misunderstanding,* by authorities of the Peronist regime. Although visa problems and other technical difficulties compelled him, after all, to pass through the Argentine capital on his way to Chile, he promptly let it be known that he intended to lecture in Buenos Aires on the subject of freedom of speech, and would refuse to submit his text for advance censorship. The easily foreseeable result was that he was unable to address an Argentine audience.

Continuing by plane across the Andes to Chile, Camus admired Santiago, nestled between the Pacific and the mountains, and offering violent colors and almond trees in bloom against a white backdrop of snow-capped peaks. The splendid mimosas and weeping willows of the Chilean countryside made him feel almost at home, and he wrote that he would not mind living there for a while under different circumstances. (Santiago at the time was living under a state of siege due to demonstrations and student riots, so that Camus was forced to deliver his lecture at the French Institute rather than at the university as planned.)

On the whole, the South American trip was a serious disappointment, marred by poor health, restrictions on his freedom of speech, and the stolidity of his audiences. The reader of the *American Journals* cannot but be struck by the weight, stress, and strain of these months abroad. The tone of the *Notebook* entries is somber and bathed in gray light, relieved by only a few spots of humor. Boarding his gray plane for the return flight to Paris on August 31, 1949, Camus was saturated with feverish perspiration and penicillin. "The trip ended in a metallic coffin, in between a mad doctor and a diplomat," the *American Journals* glumly conclude.

The published literary works of Albert Camus reveal many things about the man and writer, yet often leave the reader guessing about essential aspects of his personality and the meaning of his work. Much of what remains obscure in the novels, play, essays, and short stories is clarified and illumined by a perusal of the two volumes of *Notebooks* published after his death, supplemented by the separate volume of *American Journals* containing impressions from his lecture tours in North America in 1946 and in South America in 1949.

With rare directness and immediacy, Camus in these personal jottings from the years 1935–51 takes the reader "inside" the creative process and enables him to trace the stages of his intellectual development, the genesis and composition of his works, and the

way in which his inborn sensitivity and artistry repeatedly gained
precedence over political or utilitarian considerations. In the *Notebooks*, Camus mentions which books he himself is reading, as well
as what essays, plays, novels, and short stories he proposes to write.
From them one can gain a clear impression of the recurrent themes
and reappearing characters that stud his literary production.

Conclusion

Camus's *American Journals* end on a melancholy and foreboding note as the "metallic coffin" transports him back to France after his fatiguing South American trip and exhausting bouts with tuberculosis. Throughout his life Camus had been kept aware of his own impending death, as well as the problem of death in general, by the knowledge that the European mortality rate for lung tuberculosis remained high for his generation in spite of the introduction of "mycin" chemotherapeutic agents and antibiotic adjuvants. His untimely and unforeseen death in 1960 was, however, unrelated to the menacing pulmonary disease. Ironically and unexpectedly, it was a banal automobile accident, in which he was not even driving and which denied him even the chance to show his usual courage, that caused the entire literary world—not excluding Jean-Paul Sartre—to grieve the loss of one who had bravely confronted not only physical debilitation and the sight of his own expectorated blood, but also the horrifying experiences of World War II and the subsequent bloodbath in his Algerian homeland.

Albert Camus had called man's destiny, and his idea of historical progress, into question. He had probed the reasons and justifications for human existence, the relationship between man and his gods, between man and man. He had asked fundamental questions about the connection between politics and morality, about the intimate "I" vis-à-vis the sociopolitical "I." It is precisely because these radical questions have no clear-cut answers that it is difficult to sketch a sure portrait and distinguish the real Albert Camus from the official image. He lived both inside and outside his writings, as though unsure whether they were a comfortable place of refuge or an ensnaring trap. Even after twenty years of literary activity, he still was obsessed with the idea that his work had not yet begun.

Camus was a solid and a just man, in the human meaning of those terms. He condemned violence in all its forms, and the very idea of any totalitarian organization of life was utterly repugnant to him. In the face of every type of plague or scourge, man-made or heaven-sent, he rejected resignation, accepted only struggle, and called for total personal involvement to set an example of sacrifice. He championed unconditional resistance to all the follies that ideologies, political parties, or societies propose, recognizing, with Descartes, the need for doubt and for submission to verification of all ideas and platforms. It is his enormous personal merit to have contributed to helping men conduct themselves as free individuals, at a time when the only permitted conduct was a blind conformism, when the ideologies of Fascism, Nazism, and then Stalinism appeared to be triumphing, when the only overlying reality seemed to be the suppression of individual freedom in the name of an illusory future society. He was himself a strong militant, but for none of the political parties or organizations he so distrusted. He fervently sought a world governed by honest, capable, and willing men who would resist the temptation of absolutes and definitive solutions, who would strive instead to achieve a "relative utopia" informed by a Mediterranean sense of measure and proportion.[1]

Were Albert Camus alive today, he probably would not be pleased with the looks of the world, though he would undoubtedly rejoice at the awarding of the coveted French literary Goncourt Prize (1987) to Tahar Benjelloun, a Moroccan author writing in French, and the Nobel Prize for Literature (1988) to Najīb Mahfūz, an Egyptian author writing in Arabic; at the inauguration (1987) of the grandiose Arab cultural center in Paris; at the construction under way of a similar center in Rome; and at the proposal for a university in Alexandria, Egypt, for students of all the francophone nations of Africa. His heart would not be gladdened by the chemical and political pollution of the Mediterranean, that temple of beauty and light in which he was wont to worship. How many of the twelve countries Camus loved so deeply, and which he linked in a special, cognate relationship, are now gripped by antagonisms, strife, and acts of terrorism. The Mediterranean has become a sea of turmoil and conflict; its waters have taken on the hue of blood, glowing not with the flames of sunset but with the fire of bombs and Molotov cocktails.

Scenes of violence and desecration were as familiar to Camus as they are to us, and he had pondered deeply the contradictions and vagaries of the human condition. If he offered no conclusive answers to the human enigma, he offered understanding, comfort, and courage both to his contemporaries and to all of us who come after. The plague, he says, is still lurking somewhere, awaiting its opportunity to break out anew. But he has also created the symbol of the almond trees: "When I lived in Algiers I always patiently waited through the winter because I knew that in one night, in one single, cold and pure night in February, the almond trees of the Valley of Consuls would be covered with white flowers."

Passionate, generous, and ardent in his conduct and beliefs, the figure of this first "Mediterranean" writer recalls another sometimes misunderstood author, Niccolò Macchiavelli, who, like Camus, had "learnt to do without before he learnt to enjoy." This Renaissance Florentine, so often execrated as the incarnation of political evil, also longed for a society of good and pure men, and, like Camus, sought inspiration rather in antiquity than among his contemporaries. His two-line, versified self-portrait may serve also to sketch a part of Albert Camus:

> Io rido, e il rider mio non passa dentro:
> Io ardo, e l'arson mia non par di fore.
>
> (I laugh, and my laughter is not within me;
> I burn, and the burning is not seen outside.)

Notes

Introduction

1. Serge Doubrovsky, "Camus in America," in *Camus: A Collection of Critical Essays*, edited by Germaine Brée (Englewood Cliffs: Prentice-Hall, Inc., 1962), p. 17.

1. The Story of His Life

1. Roger Grenier, *Albert Camus. Soleil et ombre* (Paris: Gallimard, 1987). Grenier's long friendship and collaboration with Camus began during 1943–44 when the two were contributing to clandestine newspapers: Camus to *Combat* (under the pseudonym of Bauchard) and Grenier to the cultural pages of *Libertés*.
2. Roger Grenier reports that Camus's love for Tuscany was so strong that he once said: "I would like to die on the road going from Monte San Savino to Siena." Cf. Elena Guicciardi, "Camus, testa da garagista," *La Repubblica,* November 9, 1988.
3. Buzzati, with much trepidation, met Camus for the first time on the occasion of the presentation of *A Clinical Case* at the Théâtre La Bruyère in Paris in 1955. Later the timid Italian was to recall: "Thank God, [Camus] didn't look like an egghead; he looked sporty, open, a man of the people, solid, ironic, but with bonhomie; in a certain sense he looked like a garageman." Grenier, *op. cit.*, p. 247.
4. Giulia Massari, "Albert Camus, questo misconosciuto," *Il Giornale,* May 27, 1984.

2. The Stranger

1. Cf. Alberto Cavallari, "Camus vent'anni dopo," *Corriere della Sera,* January 9, 1980.
2. Jean-Paul Sartre, "An Explication of *The Stranger*," translated by Annette Michelson, in *Camus: A Collection of Critical Essays,* edited by Germaine Brée, (Englewood Cliffs: Prentice Hall, Inc., 1962), p. 110.

3. *The Plague*

1. The idea that each man carries the plague within him is found also in *The Fall*. Cf. Roger Quilliot in *Albert Camus. Théâtre, Récits, Nouvelles* (Paris: Gallimard, 1962), p. 1942.
2. Cf. the city of Hadrumète, ". . . une ville sans harmonie ni équilibre, une ville laide et macabre. . . . C'est que Hadrumète ne regarde pas la mer." (*Elissa, la reine vagabonde* [Paris: Editions Seuil, 1988] by Tunisian novelist Fawzi Mellah, reviewed by Tahar Benjelloun in *Le Monde,* July 22, 1988, p. 15.)
3. But see below, *The Wrong Side and the Right Side,* pp. 73–74.

4. *The Fall*

1. Cf. Pierre Nguyen-Van-Huy, *La Métaphysique du bonheur chez Albert Camus* (Neuchâtel: Editions de la Baconnière, 1962), p. 47.

5. *The Wrong Side and the Right Side*

1. Cf. Grenier, *Albert Camus,* pp. 47ff.

6. *Nuptials* and *Summer*

1. Parts of this chapter are reprinted, with permission of the editor, from *Critical Essays on Albert Camus,* edited by Bettina L. Knapp (Boston: G. K. Hall & Co., 1988, pp. 56–72.

7. *The Myth of Sisyphus*

1. Reported by Alberto Cavallari, "Camus vent'anni dopo," *Corriere della Sera,* January 9, 1980.

8. *Letters to a German Friend*

1. Joseph Hermet, *Albert Camus et le Christianisme* (Paris: Editions Beauchesne, 1976), p. 89.

9. *The Rebel*

1. Grenier, *Albert Camus,* p. 196.
2. Carol Petersen, *Albert Camus* (New York: Frederick Ungar Publishing

Co., 1978), p. 86: "Camus was above all an artist. Thus it would have been impossible for him to respond to the catastrophic world situation of our century except through an ideal born of the union of aesthetically detached serenity with philosophically exacting rigor, that is, specifically, the ideal of a new definition of the relations of give and take between the individual and the group of which the individual is an integral part."
3. Interview by Irene Bignardi, Venice, Summer 1987, *La Repubblica*, October 23, 1987.

10. *Reflections on the Guillotine*

1. Cf. Donald Lazere, *The Unique Creation of Albert Camus* (New Haven: Yale University Press, 1973), p. 29 passim.

11. *Caligula*

1. Albert Camus, *Théâtre, Récits, Nouvelles* (Paris: Gallimard, 1962), p. 1750.

12. *The Misunderstanding*

1. Camus, *Théâtre, Récits, Nouvelles*, p. 1793.

13. *State of Siege*

1. John Fletcher, ed. *Forces in Modern Drama: Studies in Variations on the Permitted Lie* (New York: Frederick Ungar Publishing Co., 1972), p. 141 passim.

14. *The Just Assassins*

1. Brilliantly played by Maria Casarès and Serge Reggiani in the original production at the Théâtre Hébertot on December 15, 1949.

15. *Exile and the Kingdom*

1. Cf. Rachel Bespaloff, "The World of the Man Condemned to Death," in *Camus: A Collection of Critical Essays*, edited by Germaine Brée, p. 102.

16. *Notebooks* and *American Journals*

1. Parts of this chapter are reprinted, with permission of the editor, from *Critical Essays on Albert Camus*, edited by Bettina L. Knapp (Boston: G. K. Hall & Co., 1988), pp. 56–72.

Conclusion

1. Giancarlo Marmori, "Albert Camus e il sole perduto," *La Repubblica*, February 5, 1980.

Bibliography

Books by Camus

American Journals. Translated by Hugh Levick. New York: Paragon House, 1987.

Caligula, and Three Other Plays. Translated by Stuart Gilbert. New York: Alfred A. Knopf, Inc., 1960.

Carnets. 2 volumes. Paris: Gallimard, 1962, 1964.

Essais. Introduction par R. Quilliot. Textes établis et annotés par R. Quilliot et L. Faucon. Paris: Gallimard, 1965.

Exile and the Kingdom. Translated by Justin O'Brien. New York: Alfred A. Knopf, Inc., 1963.

The Fall. Translated by Justin O'Brien. New York: Alfred A. Knopf, Inc., 1957.

A Happy Death. Translated by Richard Howard. New York: Alfred A. Knopf, Inc., 1972.

Lyrical and Critical Essays. Edited and with notes by Philip Thody. Translated by Ellen Conroy Kennedy. New York: Alfred A. Knopf, Inc., 1969.

The Myth of Sisyphus and Other Essays. Translated by Justin O'Brien. New York: Alfred A. Knopf, Inc., 1955.

Notebooks. Volume 1, 1935–42. Translated and with a preface and notes by Philip Thody. New York: Alfred A. Knopf, Inc., 1963.

Notebooks. Volume 2, 1942–51. Translated and annotated by Justin O'Brien. New York: Alfred A. Knopf, Inc., 1965.

The Plague. Translated by Stuart Gilbert. New York: Alfred A. Knopf, Inc., 1948.

The Rebel: An Essay on Man in Revolt. Translated by Anthony Bower. New York: Alfred A. Knopf, Inc., 1961.

The Stranger. Translated by Stuart Gilbert. New York: Alfred A. Knopf, Inc., 1946.

The Stranger. Translated by Matthew Ward. New York: Alfred A. Knopf, Inc., 1988.

Théâtre, Récits, Nouvelles. Préface par Jean Grenier. Textes établis et annotés par Roger Quilliot. Paris: Gallimard, 1962.

Secondary Sources

Brée, Germaine. *Albert Camus*. New York: Columbia University Press, 1964.

———, ed. *Camus: A Collection of Critical Essays*. Englewood Cliffs: Prentice-Hall, 1962.

Champigny, Robert. *Sur un héros païen*. Les Essais 93. Paris: Gallimard, 1959.

Cruickshank, John. *Albert Camus and the Literature of Revolt*. London: Oxford University Press, 1960.

Fletcher, John, ed. *Forces in Modern French Drama: Studies in Variations on the Permitted Lie*. New York: Frederick Ungar Publishing Company, 1972.

Grenier, Roger. *Albert Camus. Soleil et ombre*. Paris: Gallimard, 1987.

Hermet, Joseph. *Albert Camus et le Christianisme*. Paris: Editions Beauchesne, 1976.

Knapp, Bettina L., ed. *Critical Essays on Albert Camus*. Boston: G. K. Hall & Co., 1988.

La Postérité du Soleil. "Itinéraire" d'Henriette Grindat. Postface de René Char. Geneva: Edwin Engleberts, 1965.

La Revue des Lettres Modernes. *Albert Camus 9: La pensée de Camus*. Textes réunis par Raymond Gay-Crosier, sous la direction de B. T. Fitch. Paris: Minard, 1979.

Lazere Donald. *The Unique Creation of Albert Camus*. New Haven: Yale University Press, 1973.

Mailhot, Laurent. *Albert Camus ou l'imagination du désert*. Montréal: Les Presses de l'Université de Montréal, 1973.

Nguyen-Van-Huy, Pierre. *La Métaphysique du bonheur chez Albert Camus*. Neuchâtel: Editions de la Baconnière, 1962.

Petersen, Carol. *Albert Camus*. New York: Frederick Ungar Publishing Company, 1969.

Picon, Gaëtan. "Exile and the Kingdom." *Le Mercure de France*, May 1957. Translated by Josephine Valenza, pp. 127–31.

Quilliot, Roger. *La mer et les prisons: Essais sur Albert Camus*. Paris: Gallimard, 1956.

Thody, Philip. *Albert Camus 1913–1960*. London: Hamish Hamilton, 1961.

Index